NET WEALTH

NET WEALTH

or

Financial Literacy for Teens
(and anyone else who wants to learn about wealth)

Brian E. Rowe, CFA, CAIA

ISBN: 979-8-9908869-1-9

This book is designed to provide readers with a general overview of financial thinking and how to apply it to disciplined personal money management. It is not designed to be a definitive investment guide or to replace advice from a qualified financial planner or other professional. Investing assumes numerous risks of loss and there is no guarantee that the investment ideas suggested in the book will be profitable. Thus, the author assumes no liability of any kind for any losses that may be sustained as a result of applying the suggestions made in this book; any such liability is hereby expressly disclaimed.

Attention: Schools and Businesses
This book is available at quantity discounts with bulk purchase for educational, business, or sales promotional use. For information, please email financial-literacy@stepintopurpose.co today.

TABLE OF CONTENTS

PREFACE

A year or two out of business school, early in my career, I found myself coaching colleagues and acquaintances on basic money management skills. Most folks had no idea how they had ended up in so much debt or why their credit scores were so low or if they would ever be able to save enough for a down payment on a home. After showing them how to use various budgets, cash flow templates, loan payoff schedules and compound interest forecasts, the people I coached eventually developed strong habits and made real strides along their now more-thoughtful financial journey. I was hooked on helping and a life-long purpose for my life crystallized!

Then my wife started her own life coaching business to provide young adults with wise advice, encouragement, and guidance to work through questions about identity and to establish their own aspirational goals for achieving *real* purpose in their lives. A financial literacy module was an obvious need, so we incorporated the ideas in this book into her work with teens. This progress though left me with fundamental unanswered questions: Why is this stuff a mystery? When are teens – *anyone* really – supposed to learn all this? Why do so many *adults* lack a financial plan until it's too late or otherwise act foolishly with their money? Why do we have such a money-related retirement crisis here in the U.S.? Receiving not just a little encouragement of my *own* from her pointy shoes on my bony rear, I realized it was almost too late for us to make sure *our own kids* knew what I wanted *all kids* to learn about money, saving and investing.

The idea for a "financial literacy book" has been running around in my head like a Tom and Jerry cartoon for years; so, after procrastinating by reading every other book in the house first, this "operator's manual for money" started taking shape. I was blessed to grow up in a family that cherishes knowledge and financial wisdom, as you will see in various stories told throughout. I certainly had great mentors with plenty of examples of success before trying my own hand at various investments. I also started working and saving and investing *years* earlier than most of my peers – a habit that continues to compound benefits for my family today (foreshadowing)! This book is thus my attempt to combine early life lessons and examples along with decades of my own professional experience and the occasional commentary I lavishly poured over my kids the first fifteen years of their lives (usually during one of our board game sessions). I believe this book can help *anyone* achieve literacy about wealth!

The first nine chapters detail the most important things I believe young adults leaving high school *should* know before we parents – ceremoniously or not – shove them into the real world, financially literate or not. They need to understand why money exists, why education and experience are critical for getting the best paying jobs, how to set up a plan for spending and saving, why investing is so important and how to go about doing that. Instead of ushering our kids into debt enslavement or sheltering them from the family budget decisions, we parents *must* demonstrate good habits. Talk about your household income and expenses, show how to judiciously balance them while setting aside savings for future needs. Have monthly portfolio reviews of your own retirement assets with the kids (OK, maybe just the smaller pockets like the Roth IRA or their own Uniform Transfer to Minors Account) so they can ask questions, create their own investment thesis, practice picking stocks. Or have them help you turn over the rental for the next tenant, like my dad did with me when I was seven or eight. Or bring them along to the next Keiretsu Forum to hear a start-up's investment pitch. Once our kids participate in our own *purposeful* financial lives, we can better coax them and encourage them to dream bigger and plan how they are going to execute *their* choices in life to achieve their *own* aspirational goals.

If you are reading this as a teen, start to "gamify" your new financial literacy in real life and use the tools provided throughout the text. Spreadsheets can be confusing at first, but it really is just logic and some simple math: nothing more complicated than multiplication and division here! Share these concepts with your friends and make a pact with each other to practice the ideas presented in this book, question each other, compare bank accounts, compete a little with each other, sharpen each other like sword and stone. Start an investment club with your social peers and just explore various topics, don't worry about making money every step of the way, but seek knowledge and pursue wisdom. Don't forget to dream about all the things you can do once you have enough money and assets to stop worrying about basic needs. If you can dream up ten-, thirty- and fifty-year goals for things you want to accomplish, this book offers you the tools to get there.

Personal finance management is, like most things, mostly mental. The hard part is putting that mental knowledge – *financial literacy* – into practice as good money habits. Learn to recognize bad financial habits and commit to alter them. Create a plan and stick with the plan, but if things change (as they always do), *update* the plan and rely on the integrity of your good habits to accommodate new directions. And yes, it *is* a marathon not a sprint... there are things in this book that will take *decades* to accomplish! Also, most people find comfort in sharing the journey with someone; find a wise financial coach and ask them to keep you accountable, maybe twice a year. OK, maybe more often at first. Good coaches provide interim goals and verify you are staying on target along the way.

I am delighted when the people I have coached celebrate a win with me and explain all they had to do to make it happen – makes me all warm and cuddly inside like a kitty cat! Just remember money is not the goal; it is a tool. This book beats that drum *ad infinitum* (and probably *ad nauseum*, hat tip to Bill Gates). Use the tool to help you achieve an aggressive purpose for your life, aspire to outdo yourself and impact the greatest number of people for the greatest amount of good. Don't let a lack of financial literacy slow you down! If this book inspires you, follow-up in a few years or decades and let me know how it changed your life; I'll be stoked to hear about that journey!

For now, I'm just hopeful my own kids will read this and tell me, "Dad, you tell us this stuff *all* the time... since, like, forever ago. Besides, my trading model is crushing it this year! Go play with your kitty cat♪." Mostly because I love my kids desperately and I know this book's perspective on money, saving and investing will give them – *and you!* – the tools and habits to pursue excellence... but also because I love playing with my kitty cat!

Brian♪ Rowe, February 29, 2024

♪ Denotes (pun intended!) songs from the unofficial soundtrack listed in the appendix!

CHAPTER 1: MONEY

Money is classically called a medium of exchange which is a fancy way of saying "I'll give you this if you give me that." It should be something easy to carry and easy to use because everyone values it identically. The physical (or now electronic) media offered in exchange for something else is usually coins, bills, checks and banknotes, also called promises to pay. More recently, the term money refers to electronic credits and debits including things like cryptocurrencies and tokens, but that is another topic entirely.

MONEY' IS A TOOL

Always remember that money is a tool used to accomplish things. Employers will *buy* your time in the form of labor and *pay* you money to get things done. Sometimes you might get a few Benjamins...

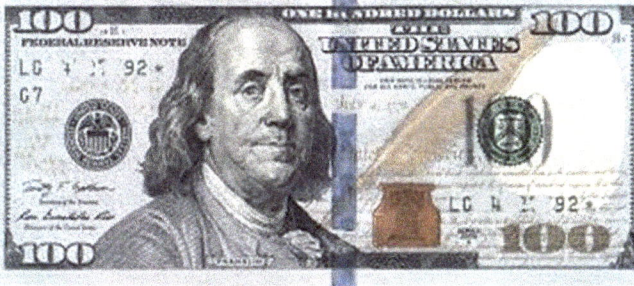

...but usually you get a pay stub, just a piece of paper listing out how many hours you worked, how many taxes you paid and what was sent to your bank account. Then you probably use your debit card or maybe a credit card or perhaps even transfer some of that amount to your favorite payment app like ApplePay, Venmo or CashApp.

Money serves as a common metric for valuing things. We will mostly refer to the U.S. dollar but for now remember that a dollar's value is constantly in flux – sometimes worth more and sometimes worth less... hopefully never worthless! So, it is wise for you and your trading partner to make sure you understand *money*.

BARTER EXCHANGE

Before money was created about 2,500 years ago, people would haul around other things they valued and try to *barter* those items in exchange for other items. For instance, if you were a farmer, you might try to trade a bushel of wheat for a new plow or a truckload of wheat for a new horse. Why? You can only eat so much wheat but there's a lot of work that goes into growing it, harvesting it and getting it ready to eat... sure would be nice to have a draft animal to help or some shiny new tools to make that work easier. Hey, why not "rent" a friend for a few days to help out? How much wheat would your friend charge you to work all day in the hot sun while getting hungry staring at all your wheat? Or what if you wanted to take a trip over a long distance because you heard from another farmer that the folks in the next country over are super hungry this year? You could probably get more than one new plow and a mule for less wheat than the local market would charge!

Or maybe you're really good at working metal and can make really cool chain mail armor; what's that worth in a barter system? You have to eat and probably need a place to sleep, store your hammers and tongs and keep a hot furnace going... um, where do you find ore and how much time do you want to spend digging it up before beating it into something useful? Things can quickly get complicated: you give the farmer a part for his plow, and he can give you wheat (bread) that you can eat and also use to pay the guy who mines and hauls the ore you need (probably have to throw in a pick and shovel for him, too). Sweet! A three-way market – life in the fast lane! (Get it? *Three*-way, fast lane... wait for it... OK, faster than a *street* market... come on, get used to the dad jokes!) I think you get the idea.

Eventually, communities created not just products but things that we *do* for others called services. What is a teacher worth? Actually, don't answer that! How about an army or a writer or someone who can sail across an ocean and (re)discover a whole new continent? Today, there is more value in traded services – things that are done by someone or something for someone else – than in actual products – tangible things you can buy, hold, use and discard. Many people are manufacturers of things or else labor somewhere within that process, but the majority of people work in services and most money today is spent on services: go out to eat dinner, or watch a movie, maybe hire a clown for your cousin's birthday party, or have a pizza delivered to your door. Leaders of government or business or education… they are all providing a service. And sometimes getting paid a lot of dough to do it! (Wait, wheat?)

<u>CURRENCIES</u>

The U.S. dollar is the primary currency for the United States. It also happens to be the most widely used currency in the world for transactions even in other countries that have their own currencies. Mostly, that has to do with the stability of government and economic productivity in the United States. The economy is a huge concept discussed in more detail toward the end of the book, but for now just think of it as all the stuff people make, buy, sell or do in exchange for money. And yes, despite all the crazy politics this nation endures, it is relatively mild compared to the broken systems of many other countries across the world. In fact, the dollar was not always trusted or valued as much as it is today – especially right after the American Revolution and even as recently as the Civil War in the last half of the nineteenth century. The dollar really began to dominate global finance in the mid-twentieth century, toward the end of World War II. Think about that: fewer than one hundred years ago the dollar was just another country's currency and even then, most currencies were tied in one way or another to gold!

Whoa! Isn't currency what electricity does, or do you mean, like, recent events? Nope. Most countries designate their own special money for use inside their country and that is called its currency. The dollar for the U.S., the yen for Japan, the yuan or renminbi in China, the peso in Mexico… and many other Latin countries even though they are mostly different kinds of pesos… yeah, it's *confusing*! and the euro is even used across most countries in Europe – so, yeah, some countries share other countries' currencies, too. The cool thing is somebody figured out how to list what every currency is worth in every other currency, so we have what is called a foreign currency exchange (FX) market. The table below is an example of a *cross-currency exchange matrix*.

Currency	USD	EUR	JPY	GBP	CHF	CAD	AUD	HKD
HKD	7.774	10.298	0.093	12.285	7.916	7.699	7.660	——
AUD	1.015	1.345	0.012	1.604	1.034	1.005	——	0.131
CAD	1.010	1.338	0.012	1.596	1.028	——	0.995	0.130
CHF	0.982	1.301	0.012	1.552	——	0.973	0.967	0.126
GBP	0.633	0.838	0.008	——	0.644	0.627	0.623	0.081
JPY	83.735	110.924	——	132.335	85.275	82.928	82.495	10.772
EUR	0.755	——	0.009	1.193	0.769	0.748	0.744	0.097
USD	——	1.325	0.012	1.580	1.018	0.990	0.985	0.129

Foreign currency is the largest market in the world even though most people only know about the stock market or maybe the commodities market. Both of *those* are smaller than even the bond market but FX is *the* biggest market, and it is never closed since someone somewhere is always awake and needs to trade their currency for a different currency in order to buy or sell something!

QUASI MONEY

The opening paragraph of this chapter mentioned cryptocurrency and tokens, so perhaps let's *spend* a little time... oh, wait, were you expecting a *dad joke* in there or something? Silly rabbit! Here's the deal. Quasi-currencies have been around a really, really long time – in fact, much longer than *paper* currency. Gold was among the first precious metals traded for other things, but it might have been silver or copper or bronze or iron... again, currency is anything everyone agrees has some value in exchange. Gold is *precious* because there is too little of it on Earth for the value people place in it, not just because it makes enchanted rings. Another example, some East Coast Native Americans used special ropes called wampum, and there is even a Pacific Islander society on the island of Yap that uses *human-sized rocks (!)* called rai used as money *today (!!)*, so sky's the limit for what qualifies as moolah. Bitcoin[*] and Ethereum and many other hundreds of quasi-currencies are all in the same vein, meaning for a group of people who agree that BTC or ETH is worth some XRP, there is an exchange of some value. The problem to solve though is how to pay for dinner, or clothes, or your mortgage with this new technology. It is possible, but it takes so many steps and at such a high cost, it just isn't worth it for most people in most situations yet today. Something to consider as we progress through this book is whether the market for a given currency is large enough and liquid enough for you to participate and eventually get back something you can spend *in exchange for* something you need or want.

THE JOURNEY BEGINS

So, as your financial literacy journey begins... don't forget to think. Use the most valuable currency you have – knowledge – and add a little bit more to that capital base (groaner pun!) as we explore how to utilize a tool – money – that *everyone on earth* uses but *few* understand. My hope is that you recognize the utility of money, what it can do for you, and how you can employ *it* to help *you* achieve an honorable and – well, *another* dad joke never killed anyone – *worthy* purpose in your life. Seriously though, money alone will not make you worthy. Just wealthy. And that's nice, too.

Money. It really is a fascinating and exciting topic! Everyone uses it. They probably think about it every day. At least once a day. Yeah, probably more often. I'm kind of a money nerd but I don't believe money is something to worship. It is something to understand and use to advance a higher-order purpose. Money can fill your pockets, but it can't fulfill your soul.

This book strives to bridge a gap I've observed since my own high school years. Today's society prioritizes teaching things it wants the next generation to do ("Obey!"); however, and curiously, money has not historically been one of those things we teach you to understand. Weird. Nobody at school taught *me* anything about deductions for taxes, or why debt is dangerous, or how to run an amortization table, or why to save for retirement, or how to set up an LLC to write off income from my lawn-mowing expenses. What gives?

Therefore... (So, what's that there for anyway?) This book is an operator's manual for money. I hope to explain in an accessible and entertaining way how to think about the value of money, how to earn money, what taxes and deductions you should expect, how to think about spending money, why it is important to save money, how to *actually* save a little money, how *cool* is compound interest anyway, unless it's in the form of debt working against you, why *investing* might be a prudent use of *some* of your *savings* and how to go about doing that, what's a credit score and how can *anyone* maximize their net wealth. I also believe it is critical for high schoolers to understand what a business is, how interest rates, inflation and demographics affect economics, why the bond and stock markets exist and how to learn about them and use them. Finally, as a glance behind the curtain, why is there such a large private market, why is that path attractive for so many companies and how should we – *should we?* – participate in private real estate, private equity, venture capital, hedge funds and angel investing? This guide strives to serve as an introduction alongside a solid grounding in budgeting and personal finance. Hopefully, it inspires your curiosity to explore the wild and constantly evolving universe of *money*!

CHAPTER 2: SCRATCHING THE SURFACE

LABOR, BUDGETS AND CAPITAL

Here are the key concepts to keep in mind for your financial literacy journey. People work, we *labor* as a way of converting our time, energy and experience into cash money: *dollah-dollah-bill*, *y'all*! Alas, the government usually *taxes* first dibs... doh! We are left with our *net earnings* or income. That's when the choices start piling up: where do I spend this cash money burning a hole in my pocket? Smart people (like you!) will develop a plan for spending *some* of their money to enjoy the fruits of their labor; *wise* people will stick with the plan! If you do this right – create an income-expense *budget* and stick with it – you will have Capital. And yes, it should be with a capital C. Capital is an asset, kind of like a friend or an employee, that will work tirelessly, and almost *effortlessly*, on your behalf to increase your net wealth. Like Tiny Troy, Capital is always working... and *Money Never Sleeps*. That was a shameless plug for a movie about money, sorry.

This section and the following chapters introduce some new terms, tools and actions that are critical to understand and utilize, put into practice, make part of your being... imbue. The suggestions made are a great starting point, but feel free to adjust the targets to your ability and your current status. Things like "save $1,000 as an emergency fund" may seem outlandishly difficult; fine, start with $500 or even $100 and then work methodically, if more slowly, toward the stated goal. Eventually, you will develop the correct *habit* and *that* is the critical take-away, not the actual dollar amount goal. Habit is everything in personal finance. Make good habits; break-up with bad ones... same advice goes for friends, too, come to think of it.

```
              EARNING
                 ↑
                 |
                 |
                 |
 SAVING  ←———————+———————→  INVESTING
                 |
                 |
                 |
                 ↓
             SPENDING
```

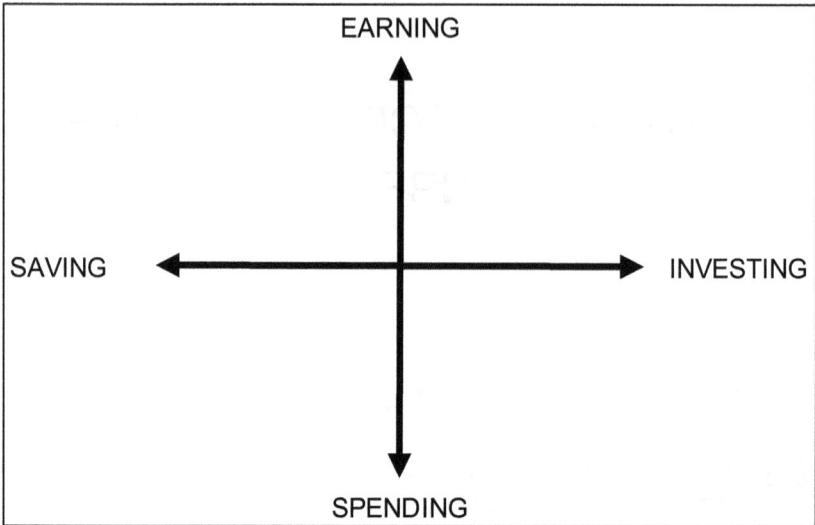

Simplicity in form and function: this sums up the input (your earnings) and alternatives related to personal finance.

Earning and *Spending*. Most of us are seemingly born with an ability to spend, but *earning* money must be learned and nobody really enjoys it. Oh, they may enjoy doing the thing that accomplishes it – acting in a movie is *exciting*, and sometimes pays pretty well. Being a Founder or CEO can be the expression of your life's purpose, thus totally fulfilling... and hey, probably pays the bills, too. Most of us, though, are *worker bees*, employees who labor for a periodic paycheck. All of us have expenses. How *many* bills you have and how *much* you *spend* must be considered ahead of time and managed ruthlessly or else you will never achieve your financial goal, nor your purpose, which is almost definitely *not* a *financial thing* at all.

Saving and *Investing*. This is a little trickier: if you spend everything you earn, you don't *save* anything and can't pay for things when you need them. That's a bummer, especially if you're hungry. Or have no shirt and shoes. Or no warm bed. If you spend *less than* you earn, you can save some money to spend when you need it and haven't been paid yet. If you *save* more than you need for the foreseeable future, let's say one year, you could *invest* in other people and have them pay you even more than you "gave" them. This last bit is called letting your Capital... and people who *didn't* learn to save their money... *work for you*. This is why you bought this book or took this class: so that when you look back on your life, *you* were the people who *saved*, then *invested* money rather than *spent* the money you *earned* and had to *borrow debt* to survive. Gold star! And sparkles!

EARNING MONEY

There may be no limit to how much you *earn*, but you should consider your earnings as a definite ceiling on how much you *spend* (i.e., always plan to spend less than you earn). Any money you can *save* should be mentally set aside for that purpose and used only for emergencies – sadly, emergencies happen all the time, so plan for them by setting aside savings to cover the cost when they do happen. Eventually, you will save so much money, you can begin to look at *investing* some of those savings. Investing is a way to increase your earnings without doing more labor. For example, I earned and saved diligently as a teenager, so I was able to invest early and often enough that I didn't have to labor (work) once I turned forty... but I still *choose* to work, I enjoy it! It's nice to have options; understanding money will give you a ton of options throughout life (yes, there's a pun there, but a little too early). So, buckle up, let's get busy and *make some money*!

FROM BEGGING TO INHERITING

There are lots of ways to make money. Dude on the corner in shabby clothes, looking forlorn (google it) but, *sweet!* cardboard artwork that says, "Hey buddy, spare a dime?" This is a classic role in society, though in some countries it's outright illegal. Regardless, begging♪ or panhandling or busking is actually one way to earn money. Probably not the highest hourly payout, let's be honest; still, people do it, have always done it, and it's not at all difficult.

Seeking *handouts* or applying for *welfare* is our society's attempt to separate self-imposed *pauperism* from unfortunate, and hopefully temporary, *poverty*. There is a whole philosophy here that is beside the point (or maybe it's a *bigger* point we just can't fully address here) but please recognize tragedy *can* lead to desperate outcomes (e.g., homelessness) that look exactly like situations resulting from poor decisions (e.g., addictions, leading to mental illness, leading to crime, etc.). There are many outlets for financial charity that help families in need and individuals escape poverty; these are worthy and admirable

> My son played guitar and sang songs on street corners, at public markets and outside restaurants for years before he was even ten – loved it! Had a great time doing it! Made great money and it forced him to practice without even complaining! So don't think I'm dissing busking[j], just maybe not a lifetime of it!

options for people who need help *bootstrapping* themselves to a better situation.   Please consider supporting these efforts, organizations and civic societies who do purposeful work to help society. If not *just* with your money, then with your time, energy and intellect! Hey, that almost sounds like a ready-made purpose!

Those of you pursuing higher education will be thrilled to learn there are organizations and individuals who offer *grants* to achieve those goals. It's almost like someone *gives* you money to go to school and get a degree! And yes, that's exactly what this is: *free money*! Many books have been written to show you who to ask and how to apply for money via this route. Realize it is a possibility, think about why the possibility exists and whether you qualify as a potential recipient. Later in life, when *you* are financially independent and wistfully recalling this intro course on money, consider donating to or starting your own grantmaking foundation and teach the next generation to also be generous and thoughtful with their resources.

Some of you will *inherit* more than an older sibling's clothes when your parents or grandparents pass away. Quite a few of the wealthiest families in the world achieved that status through inheritance... life's not fair either but whatever, I'm not bitter. Perhaps you can set a goal today to pass on a stack of bills and precious gems to your kids and grandkids and maybe a little to the author of that great financial literacy book you read decades ago... what a great idea! Generational wealth, as it's called, doesn't happen all that often and it makes surprisingly little news when it does happen. Weird? Not really, since wealthy families know how to pass on their wealth by way of a legal arrangement called a *trust* that does not have to be publicized unlike the legal process of a will through probate. Again, tons of already-written books on this, worthwhile for you to explore in a couple of decades, depending on changes to the tax code, etc., but everyone should know it is one way of earning money or at least starting off with some money. And that would make everything else we cover much easier. Or harder: most generational wealth is squandered within three generations since the inheritors seldom take the time to learn the lessons presented in this book. They forget to become financially literate with the money they start with, so they frequently end up losing it all!

PART-TIME LABOR

Let's go out on a limb here and say *all of you* at some point during your life will have a part-time job', where you work less than 40 hours per week. Some of you may already tutor your peers for some spending cash or lifeguard at a community pool during the summer or mow neighborhood lawns (I did!); however, the most popular route for teens to begin working is in the service industry which basically means restaurants and retail shops. These are usually easy jobs showing diners to the table, taking orders, delivering food, stocking inventory and ringing up purchases at the cash register. My first "real job" was as a bus boy and dishwasher at a deli for something like $5.35 an hour... I loved it! The job... the bosses, not so much.

Regardless of what kind of part-time job you get, there are different ways to get paid. (Cue the soundtrack for They Might Be Giants' *Minimum Wage!*) I was paid a minimum amount for each hour I worked set by the federal government and sometimes a higher amount set by the state in which I lived; this is probably the most typical setup. There is also a method called *commissions* that is more common in a professional sales organization: Nordstrom suits and shoes salespeople might get paid a small percentage of each sale they make; car salespeople have a *graduated scale* of increasing percentages the higher the sales price of a car over some internal target. Another method is to pay someone a *fixed fee* for each unit they make or sell, sometimes referred to as *piecework*. For example, you might get paid 25 cents by your older sibling for each duct tape wallet you make for their friends. Or for each box of cookies you sell at the mall, the company pays you $1 regardless of how much each customer pays per box. Or perhaps you get paid $25 for each student who attends your tutoring class, even though *they* pay $100 to attend. The main idea in all these methods is to compensate you for spending your time, energy and expertise to exchange something of value with a buyer who pays money for the product or service. The money they pay must be enough to cover your compensation and all the costs that go into making that product or service available to purchase... and hopefully generate a profit. We will cover the details of *business* in a later chapter since it is so fundamental to understand so you can make tons of money over your lifetime.

THE GIG ECONOMY

A more recent way to make money is referred to as the *gig economy*. Think of anyone driving for Uber, Lyft, DoorDash or someone who rents out a room in their house through AirBNB: they are participating in the gig economy *on the side* to make a little extra money even though they may have another job, possibly even in addition to a full-time job. In most of these cases, it's hard to actually make enough to cover the expenses (for example, the gas, insurance, wear-and-tear on your car, speeding tickets[*], accident repairs, car washes, etc.) of providing the service, not to mention the hourly payment for your time. Find someone who does this and ask them to tell you how much they made on average over three- or six months. Then ask them how much they spent on all the things they needed to make that money. Their take-home profit is usually much less than they think!

GAMING THE SYSTEM

For most part-time jobs, the real juice is intended to be what are called *tips,* the spare change and bills from generous customers who leave gratuity for great service. Once I graduated from dishwasher to waiter/server in the restaurant business, I hustled to make sure my customers got their cold drinks fast, food hot and all their requests met with a friendly smile and witty banter so they would feel obligated to leave a big tip! Sometimes people leave tips of 5% or 10% of the total bill and that's nice, but the folks who got extra attention from their host, salesperson or server often left tips of 20%, 30% and (one time) even 100%! If you are serving five tables and each bill is $100 and they all gave you 20% tips, that's $100 in your pocket. It probably took an hour for them to eat and clear out, so you made $100 in addition to the minimum wage for that hour! Turn over your tables four times during your shift and that's $400 for the day! Anyway, that's why restaurants pay minimum wage and why it's better to work at really nice/expensive restaurants and hopefully have lots of tables and people that eat fast. But you still have to do a great job and make their experience worth a big percentage tip.

In addition to, or instead of, tips many industries offer things called perks, short for perquisites, when working there. In restaurants you might get half off any food you order whether you worked that day or not (e.g., one free meal $15 or less at the end of a shift). At a clothing store, you might get 35%-50% off anything in the store. Some car salespeople get to take a car from the lot to drive to and from work. Some places like Brookstone, Cranium or toy shops might give you a free massager, slinky or radio-controlled gadget to play with and keep – these are called spiffs or merch, short for merchandise. I worked for a trade show production company for a while and most of the clients who rented booth space from us would give out things like pens, memory sticks, iPods or lava lamps and I'd usually end up with a trunk full of junk to impress my friends. Another place I worked during college ordered lunch for all its employees... *every stinkin' day*!

Whatever industry you end up working in, you should consider the perks and what value those might have for you. Big family with lots of mouths to feed: take free or discounted food home from the restaurant or grocery store after your shift. Love the drip at Nike, Tommy Bahama or Psycho Bunny: get a job as salesperson, inventory stocker or janitor. Maybe you like to travel, so find a job that requires you to fly to different cities or countries *on the company's dime*!

One last thing, and probably the most important idea here, is to always *learn something* where you work. You are giving them your time, energy and expertise so be sure to increase your knowledge and level of skills. Figure out how the company makes money and when you help them make more money, they will usually pay you even more. In customer-facing roles, learn how to meet people, engage them in conversation and develop trusting relationships; those are skills everyone needs to succeed in society. As you grow into an authentic and genuine builder of relationships, those skills will be worth *more* than anything an employer can pay you.

MILITARY CAREERS

Most countries have a professional military with life-long professionals who manage it. They didn't just apply and get the job after reading a bunch of war novels and watching *Jack Ryan* or *A Few Good Men*. Rather, they probably joined one of the armed services (Army, Navy, Air Force, Marines, Coast Guard or National Reserves, for example) right out of high school or college and worked their way up from the bottom. Apart from the hard work required to learn all the skills of soldiering, this can be a highly rewarding career track for many people. And they teach you really useful and sometimes *top secret!* stuff about technology, techniques and procedures like security and logistics. The pay may not *sound* great, but the benefits are usually pretty fly: On-base housing is free! Meals are free! Clothes are free! Travel to foreign countries is free! Guns and bullets are free! Combat pay is *tax free!* Medical insurance is free! You get a pension and full retirement benefits after only twenty years! Seriously, though, a career in the military can expose you to brilliant people driven to excel, can put you on the cutting edge of research and technology, and can position you to serve the needs of millions of other people in massive ways. Give it some serious thought and talk to folks who have served[3] to learn more about this career path.

ENTREPRENEURSHIP

Entrepreneurship is a Frenchy, er, fancy way to say "build your own business and work for yourself." It doesn't necessarily mean making some novel product or writing wicked code that does something nobody ever did before; it *can* lead to that, but usually doesn't. If you open a dry cleaner and operate it yourself or hire people to run it, that's entrepreneurship. If you write a magazine and publish it – hard copy or online – and sell ads or get people to subscribe, that's it too. You could even organize a sports league, sign up a few dozen teams, rent a few fields or gyms and host a tournament with entry fees per team to win a championship prize, sell tickets and concessions... that's entrepreneurship! What do you think the NFL or UFC was before it was professional?

If you have a passion and an idea how to promote that passion to others, you should seriously explore some of the hundreds of books on entrepreneurship and surround yourself with others who share your passion or at least recognize the potential of your idea. This is the starting point for most of the wealthiest people in the world: they had an idea, worked tirelessly to promote that idea, built a business around it and ultimately sold some of it to someone else (usually another business). It's a fascinating journey, filled with a roller-coaster of success and failure along the way. Read biographies of successful entrepreneurs and *founders*; dream about fixing a huge need; change the world with your passionate ideas for a great business!

FULL-TIME LABOR

Now, most of us do not have that level of passion or energy or willingness to take financial risks. That's OK, too! Thankfully, there are millions of businesses out there that need our labor. Here in the U.S., we have adopted a typical 40-hour work week, usually eight hours each of five days during the week[*]. That changed a bit getting through Covid-19, but most adults tend to go into offices or shops or research facilities or commute in their vehicles Monday through Friday, work about eight hours with a few breaks here and there for lunch or coffee or picking up kids from school, etc. They may work more or fewer than eight hours on a given day, but the employer's expectation is about 40 hours of your productive time, energy and expertise each week.

HOW TO EARN *MORE* MONEY

Early in your career you probably don't have much expertise or knowledge about the job so employers pay you a little less but spend time and resources teaching you about the business so you can do your job more effectively. Again, we will go into more detail about why businesses exist, how they are structured and why it works this way, but the general idea is to coordinate the inputs of labor (you, your coworkers) and capital (computers, office space, contracts and other resources) to produce something of value for others to purchase. Your labor is part of that machine, and you get paid an annual *salary* and *benefits* to do your part. The business itself – rather, its owners –

hope to earn a profit after paying you and all the other expenses of the business.

To get any high-paying career job, you will need to prove your value to the employer, usually in the form of an education, knowledge or experience. Lots of ways to get those skills, especially if you have already been working in the industry. This is called bootstrapping your way into experience, lifting yourself up by pulling on your own bootstraps is an old metaphor. By working in the industry as a teenager, you may have learned some things about running a restaurant and how to order inventory for the Christmas sales season or how to rotate stock in the grocery store to sell stuff before it expires, thus lowering costs for your employer which makes you more valuable to them. Remember, always pay attention in any job you have, learn from both customers and bosses. This helps you demonstrate to your employer that they should hire you, again and again into higher roles, give you more responsibility and pay you more. Experience is one of the easiest ways to get the *next* full-time, better paying job. After each week, jot down something memorable you learned in a journal and review that journal every three months.

Another track to making more money is attending a technical college or trade school. You have to pay these companies a kind of tuition or annual fee, but they will provide you with teachers and resources to learn a specific skill that is in demand by other employers. If you're ever home sick, actually sick, though, not playing hooky from school or work, and end up watching day-time television – *ugh!* – you will see ads for these kinds of schools. They teach you how to draw blood (phlebotomist), diagnose car engine problems (mechanics), fix air conditioners or appliances (repair technicians) or weld plumbing lines and work with electrical utility connections. There are many tasks and jobs that require human hands and some interaction with people – again, all skills you *can* learn by doing them in a part-time job – but they may require some specific learning of procedures.

On the job training and technical or trade schools often provide an environment that makes it easy to learn how to do these jobs correctly. In many cases, they also help you get your first job with employers who recruit from these schools. The skills education can take anywhere from a few months to a couple of years to learn and the costs vary from a few hundred dollars per class up to thousands of dollars for specific certifications that prove you are a *journeyman* or *master* or some other level of technical proficiency. The higher the proficiency level, the higher the salary you may be able to demand. Unions often accomplish the same thing.

Junior colleges, often called community colleges', usually offer basic post-secondary (i.e., high school) education. These are great places to get some of the courses required by universities or state colleges out of the way without paying nose-bleed tuition fees. These college-level courses are usually taught by professional teachers who may have first held a career job in the field. I took some computer classes one summer as a tweenager from instructors who helped on DARPA projects at Bell Labs and Texas Instruments by coding software in ancient languages called Pascal, Fortran and COBOL... could've led me to work at Microsoft or Amazon when those were still start-up companies, doh! Anyhoo, each class you take and pass gives you a certain number of *credits* that are usually transferable to universities if you decide to keep going; otherwise, you can just take all the different classes that interest you and it doesn't cost all that much, usually a few hundred dollars per class.

If you discover you enjoy a certain track, like computer science or engineering or business or medicine, then you can parlay your excellent grades in these classes into a cool job doing what you enjoy! Most people though take enough *required courses* to complete what is called an *associate degree* which means you know enough stuff to be proficient at a lot of things, but you are not an expert or specialist in anything. Many folks who go this route have an eye on getting into a four-year university without paying those first two years of high fees, or they didn't have a high enough GPA (grade point average) in high school to get accepted to the university they wanted. Again, this is one way to show that university that you are good enough for them to accept you into their (probably harder but more prestigious) degree program in your field of interest.

Universities are highly regarded by most employers for producing graduates of their four- or five-year degree programs in specific fields. Employers recognize that the amount of knowledge acquired by studying and achieving high GPA's along with completing the rigorous requirements to receive a *bachelor's degree* has historically correlated well with employees who perform well in their jobs. It's not just about grades though. It takes commitment, determination, drive, discipline and some social skills to get through four years of study and pass all those tests and learn how to think. Universities also require students to take courses outside a narrow academic track to hopefully produce more well-rounded or generally knowledgeable citizens. While the main focus is and should be acquisition of knowledge demonstrated by good grades, don't forget the people you meet during these years, toiling alongside you to learn the same stuff, are probably the same people who will be your lifelong friends and business associates and colleagues. And, most people who have lots of smart friends also end up making lots of money. Hmmm...

The vast majority of employers want people with bachelor's degrees, but some need folks who go even further and achieve post-graduate education resulting in a *master's degree*, for example a Master's in Business Administration (MBA), or a *doctorate*, also called a PhD. Other specialty education tracks result in an MD, medical doctorate for the medical field, or a JD, juris doctorate for attorneys in the legal field. Yes, there are other specialty degrees, but these are the most popular. The key takeaway here is: more education typically leads to higher-paying careers. That education takes longer and is more expensive up-front, but those who excel in their studies are typically highly sought-after by employers and usually offered ridiculous amounts of money and benefits with opportunities to earn even more by owning a piece of the companies who hire them. Or they leave after gaining a few years' experience in the real world and build their own businesses and make even more money.

The last category of educational advancement to touch on is called professional certification. Many industries recognize their professionals who can demonstrate or qualify their knowledge and experience by sitting for various exams and achieving their industry's *professional certification*. Accountants work for a few years and study (sometimes on the job but usually after hours at home) to sit for a CPA exam and earn a designation that shows they are a Certified Public Accountant. Investment advisors who manage investment money for individuals often pursue a CFP, Certified Financial Planner, or a CFA designation as a Chartered Financial Analyst. There are dozens of professional designations, but the common thread is immediate recognition by potential employers that the individual went the extra mile to demonstrate a commitment, dedication and expertise in their professional development[2].

Each of these steps – technical college, associate degree, bachelor degree, master's and PhD, professional certification – typically results in a step-up in the amount of salary or potential benefits you can earn *each year* during your career. The more money you earn, the more you can buy or save or invest. Earning money is just the beginning of our journey though. Now you must plan how to use that money, how to save that money and how to invest that money. Remember, money is just a tool. It provides you with more options in life to enjoy more things and experiences or do more for others, but it is not the end goal of life. Your life has a purpose and money can help you achieve that purpose, so what plans will *you* make for your earnings to accomplish the most with your life?

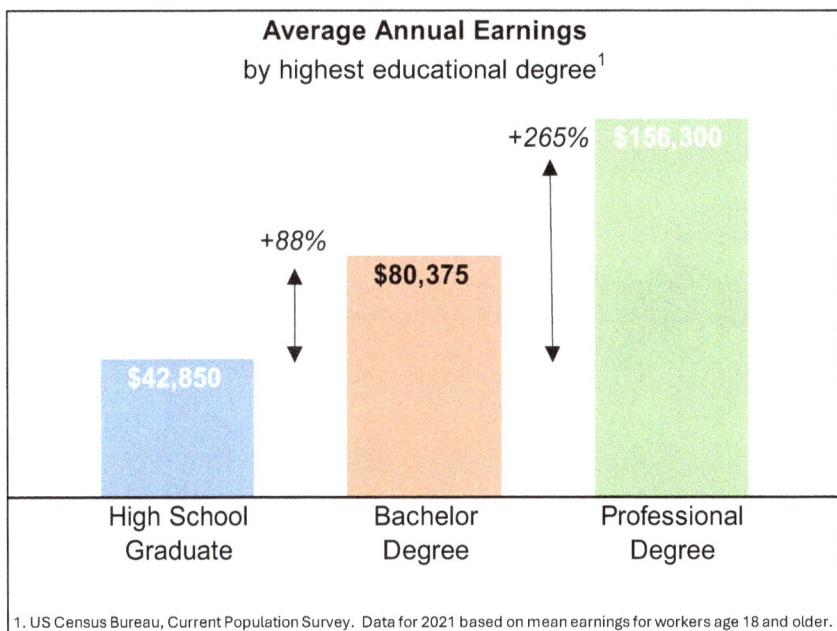

Average Annual Earnings
by highest educational degree[1]

+265% $156,300

+88% $80,375

$42,850

High School Graduate   Bachelor Degree   Professional Degree

1. US Census Bureau, Current Population Survey. Data for 2021 based on mean earnings for workers age 18 and older.

CHAPTER 3: THE PAYCHECK, TAXES AND DEDUCTIONS

In this world, nothing is certain except death and taxes.
– Benjamin Franklin, 1790

Cheery thought, eh? So, now you are a working stiff, nine-to-five, laboring in the salt mines of the economy, a whip on the back and an ogre for a boss. But hey, you get the weekend to yourself! Except, what's this!? Who is this IRS♪... and why are they taking my money!? What the... FICA!? Security for Social what!? Medicare is for old folks, right!? Welcome to taxes and deductions from your gross income... Argh! Piracy!

FROM GROSS INCOME TO NET INCOME

Let's go through each of the sections in the example "advice of deposit" or paycheck stub at the end of this chapter. Gross income is "the amount you *thought* you were earning" per hour, per sale, per week or whatever. Most full-time workers get a paycheck every two weeks (bi-weekly) or twice a month (semi-monthly), or even once a month. The paycheck used to be a physical check attached to the statement of earnings and deductions that we would physically detach, drive to the bank and deposit or else cash it. We will cover banking in more detail later, but almost everyone will have to open a bank account to deposit money and to pay for things by taking out cash, writing checks or using a debit card. Today, employers will typically sign you up on your first day of employment for *direct deposit* and your "net pay" will be deposited directly into your bank account. You will just get the statement either in the mail, emailed to you or available for download. You should read that statement every time you get one and understand where all your money is going. If you see "Exempt" it usually means you are not allowed to earn overtime regardless how many hours you work in a day or week; the "rate" reflects your annual salary. There are *elections and allowances* that determine how much will be deducted for taxes before you even get a penny of your pay!

FEDERAL INCOME TAX (FIT)

Federal Income Tax is typically withheld from your paycheck and paid by the employer to the Internal Revenue Service (IRS) on a quarterly basis for each employee. It is a way for the government to ensure it gets paid the tax you are likely to owe without chasing you down to pay it. Makes sense: it is much easier to chase down a few million businesses withholding taxes for hundreds of millions of individuals than to chase down each individual. Instead, now YOU have to file an annual "tax return" to get any amount of overpaid taxes sent back to you; this puts you in their system and if you don't file one year, they'll suspect you are cheating and *then* chase you down.

There are *thousands* of books written, basically every year since the tax laws change so often, on how to minimize your taxes. But really, after you start making $50,000 annually, just hire a CPA or get a TurboTax software program to do it for you. It is so complicated and confusing – *by design!* However, you *can* tell your employer to withhold a specific amount of taxes from each paycheck by fiddling with the *allowances* on your hiring paperwork, typically referred to as a Form W4. The higher the number, the lower the withholding; but keep in mind, if you owe too much at the end of the year, the IRS may assess a *penalty* and interest for *underpayment*. Again, this usually will not be a problem for you unless you are making quite a bit of money each year and at that point, it would be wise to hire a professional to advise you.

SOCIAL SECURITY TAX

FICA (Federal Insurance Contributions Act) is the line item associated with Social Security (SS), a federal program started in the first half of the 20th century to provide a monthly "benefit" or payment to eligible citizens after they are too old to work. It started out as a small dollar amount to *supplement* savings for older folks or spouses who never worked, but it has grown over the decades to become the primary financial support for pretty much every retiree in the country. The basic idea is that each worker sets aside an amount of money from each paycheck that the government promises to pay back to you after you retire. So far so good; not sure why we need a huge bureaucracy to make this work, but that's what we have. The mandated rate is more than 12% of gross annual earnings (up to a maximum of ~$170,000); your employer is usually responsible for paying half and you are responsible for paying half. If you are self-employed, you lucky entrepreneurs, you get to pay the whole amount because you are working for yourself. A savings rate of 12% times $170,000 is $20,400 *per year* in retirement savings, right? You wish.

MEDICARE TAX

Medicare is, yes, federally sponsored medical insurance for older people who have retired from the workforce, thus they are no longer covered by an employer-sponsored medical plan. By the way, you *must* apply for Medicare when you turn something like 65 years old even if you have not worked long enough to qualify for Social Security. If you don't apply, even if you don't need it, the government will assess a *10% premium penalty* for each year you fail to apply, and your potential Social Security benefits can be withheld to pay for "dues" you haven't been paying along the way... but I digress. Bottom line: you and your employer pay into Medicare (at almost 3%) and Social Security (actually 12.4%) while you are working, with the expectation that you are *paying forward* for things you will need when you can no longer work. In reality, this tax is paid into "programs" that pay millions of other people taking benefits today[♪]; you are *not* contributing to *your personal* account that you will eventually use up for yourself or your family. This is unsustainable and will likely fail before you receive any of the promised benefits, not to mention the lost potential for earning a return on those savings. So, as financially literate earners, save and invest in anticipation of supporting yourself rather than rely on a government promise. Maybe your generation can fix the existing broken systems bloated by bureaucracy. Good luck.

Here is a very thin silver lining: The earnings base for Social Security and Medicare taxes can usually be reduced by saving your own money into a retirement plan (how generous!) since you are basically doing what they are supposed to do – saving and investing for a monthly income after you can't or don't want to work any longer. If you earned the theoretical max income of $170,000 but saved $23,000 into a retirement savings plan, which we explore below, then the 15%+ FICA tax is only assessed on the remaining $147,000 of earnings. Federal taxes are assessed on the amount of earnings left over after even more deductions for things covered below. Bottom line: diverting more of your income into pre-tax deductions *today* allows you to pay fewer *taxes* today and maximize *future* wealth for tomorrow... something like 40 or 50 years of tomorrow.

STATE AND LOCAL INCOME TAX

OK. Some of you live in *states* that want their pound of flesh, too! In that case, you will also have state income taxes withheld by your employer and paid to your state government. Similarly to the federal category, you will probably have some options to manage the amount they withhold based on various state-level allowances and filing status (married, blind, lots of kids, whatever). The amount states take varies anywhere from zero (AK, FL, NV, NH, SD, TN, TX, WA and WY) up to almost 20% in places like New York, Connecticut and California... a few places allow you the privilege of paying *city* income taxes as well. Curiously, those highest-taxed states and cities also often boast some of the highest average incomes and real estate property costs in the country... hmmm. Interesting.

HOURS AND EARNINGS

A work week is eight hours for each of five days, 40 hours total, so the pay period works out to 80 hours for two weeks – that's about 2,080 hours a year, but you don't actually have to *work* all those hours! Most companies offer paid holidays – you don't have to work but you still get paid! Sometimes employers allow more than just federal holidays and some "float" depending on the employer's discretion, usually the day before or after a major holiday like Easter or Independence Day and you can choose when to take them. Most employers also offer vacation: you pick when to take a certain number of days off from work but still get paid as though you showed up. Usually, employers make you earn vacation time: you must work something like ten or twelve hours to earn one hour of vacation time;

other employers are less strict about it. Occasionally, sick time is also accrued; you don't get paid when you call in sick after that balance is used up. Finally, most employers will contribute to a healthcare plan or offer a Health Savings Account (HSA) for you to use as you see fit. Those contributions are considered "imputed income" and shown as part of your earnings.

BENEFITS AND DEDUCTIONS

Then you get to categories of compensation that aren't truly earnings *per se* but that most people consider valuable, so they are called benefits. Usually, you get to elect whether to participate in them and to what extent you want to take part (i.e., how much of your paycheck goes into them). The retirement savings fund is *the most important:* variably called a 401k or 403b since that's the section of the IRS code that describes them, but also a Keogh Plan, SEP-IRA or Savings Plan. This is money that *your employer* is putting aside for you', and you can control how it is invested within the parameters of the employer-sponsored plan. More detail on this in just a bit, for now make a mental note to *maximize* this benefit referred to as the *employer retirement contribution match*!

Flexible Spending Accounts (FSA) are specially designated funds that you may be allowed to set aside before paying taxes on them to pay for things like dependent/childcare expenses or healthcare. It ties in with health savings accounts that may be sponsored by your employer. It's nice to be able to pay for things with money that hasn't been taxed, but if you put too much into an FSA and fail to use it by the end of the tax year, *it disappears*, and you never get it back. So, plan for things like eyeglasses, dental work, doctor visits and surgeries. Find out ahead of time how much you might spend *next year* and set that aside in the FSA because it results in something like a 15%-30% savings by avoiding taxes.

Most employers today do not cover 100% of your medical insurance cost like they used to do, so you have to pay some of it. The amount you pay is considered a pre-tax benefit *cost*, so you do not have to pay taxes on that. An individual pays less to cover just themselves; it costs more to provide medical coverage for a spouse who might still be in school or currently out of work. Then, once you have a gaggle of kids, you will want to pay a little more to make sure they have healthcare coverage, too. If two spouses are working, figure out which one has the more generous health coverage plan offered by their employer and use it to cover the family – especially if their employer still covers 100% of the cost! Group Term Life Insurance is another benefit: if you become disabled or die while employed, you or your family can get paid a monthly or lump sum amount since you can't work if you're unconscious or dead. The employer will show you how much that benefit is worth – they are paying the premium for the insurance coverage, after all – and you probably get taxed on it as though it were actual income. If you want to learn more about gaming the "benefits system" there are jobs in benefits management as part of the human resources (HR) department in large corporations. They might even have a professional certification or designation that you could "study for" and learn how to maximize the benefits offered by your employer or negotiate better to have them offered to you.

There may be other minor deductions *after-tax* for things like additional life insurance or employer-required uniforms or even building parking and fitness clubs and such. Basically, anything taken out of your paycheck before you get paid should be detailed on your pay stub. You should verify everything looks like you expected it to, that all the totals are right, the correct amounts are being calculated and withheld, the amount that went into your bank account is the amount printed on your statement and *ask questions* if something doesn't make sense! Make a game out of predicting what your net pay will be and how much vacation time balance you will have next paycheck. To me, the best number is the total set aside for retirement – I love watching that figure go up by the amount I'm putting away as well as by the amount my employer is contributing on my behalf. Let's spend more time digging into these powerful tools for accumulating wealth!

RETIREMENT PLANS

This is so central to financial literacy: you *must* learn what they are, why they exist and how to maximize your retirement savings plan. A hundred years and more ago, companies offered their employees a promise called a *pension*. If the employee promised to work for a salary for thirty years or so, the company would continue to pay them a generous portion of their salary even after they retired from the company. It was a pretty good deal for both parties: the employer didn't have to pay as much *today* for the employee, who would continue to receive most of their salary *tomorrow* after they couldn't work anymore. In life, expenses continue even after we can no longer earn an income by working. This was one way to solve that problem, but most companies today are no longer offering pensions because they realized what an expensive promise it is since people live so long!

Social Security has been another experiment to try and solve the earnings/spending conundrum, but problems with this system are on the horizon and no easy fix exists. Some good books have been written on this topic; basically, there are too *many* people retired and earning benefits while too *few* people are paying into the program. (Really, the problem was a failure to wisely invest those early contributions to the program, so there was no compound interest earned; and yes, there is much more detail on *that* in a later chapter!)

Workers – you! – must set aside a portion of earnings today in anticipation of the time when they can no longer work or choose not to work. How much you set aside today and for the next 30 or 40 years that you *can* earn money will determine how much you can spend without running out of money when you can *no longer* earn money. Retirement savings plans are critical to understand since they are needed to accomplish this goal.

The IRS allows individuals to set aside a maximum of about $23,000 each year from their earnings into a qualified employer sponsored plan called a 401k at most for-profit companies or 403b for most non-profits like schools, hospitals, colleges, or municipal government entities. This amount is called the employee contribution. You don't pay federal taxes on the amount you or your employer set aside today. Why would they allow this? Because they expect it to be a *much bigger* amount in the future as you earn *returns* on that money for decades. The tax will be owed when you are required to start taking what are called *distributions* from the future balance of your investments.

MATCHING AND VESTING, NOT INVESTING

Employers are encouraged, by the IRS and by competitive market forces of other employers, to *match* a portion of their employees' contributions to the retirement plan. Sometimes it's dollar-for-dollar that *you* contribute up to a maximum dollar amount, say $7,500, *matched* by the employer. So, if you contribute $10,000 of the maximum $23,000 allowed, then your employer will match the first $7,500 and you end up with an investable amount of $17,500... in just the *first year* of participating in the retirement plan! Usually, companies have a scale for matching contributions, something like 50% of the first 5% of your salary and 25% of the rest up to a maximum of 10% of your salary. Regardless of the policy set by the employer, you should always try to set aside, or *contribute,* the maximum allowed by the IRS since this will maximize the amount of the employer match. It's also a great discipline for you to live on less than you potentially earn and allows you to set aside more to invest for retirement.

If your employer doesn't match, you should make some noise about that and start looking for a different employer who does match. Or maybe even find one who offers a pension, which is like a match but you don't have to contribute anything except time as an employee. There is one catch: in order to keep *all* the money your employer matches, you may have to spend a minimum number of years working there, called a *vesting period,* something like five years, and you only *vest* in the matching contributions at 20% each year. You manage how the money is invested in the interim, but if you quit that job before you are *fully vested* the employer is allowed to keep the *unvested* portion of their matching contributions.

OK, so let's say after one year, you have set aside $10,000 and your employer added $7,500 into a 401k plan. Plans typically offer a default investment option – like a mutual fund that invests half of the money in stocks/equities and half of the money in bonds/fixed income. Some plans offer fancy products called Lifestyle Funds or Target Date Retirement Funds: these all have a feature called a *glide path* toward retirement that will shift the allocation between stocks and bonds slowly toward bonds as you get older. The theory is to take *more risk* when you're young by remaining mostly invested in equities which go up and down a lot more than fixed income which goes up and down less but may have a lower expected rate of return than equities. We'll get more into these concepts later of course, but the idea is to *gain exposure* to the investment markets so your capital – in this case retirement plan assets – is working for you to earn a return.

There is usually a dozen or more investment options for you to choose from in each company's retirement plan and by the end of this book, you'll have an idea where you'll want to invest.

Let's keep going with our example and think ahead! In year two, you're feeling more confident, so you increase your contributions to the max: $23,000 from your pre-tax earnings and you get another $7,500 from your employer. That's $30,500 just in year two alone! Added to the first year's $17,500 and – before we even *think* about the returns on that first-year investment, you're up to $48,000 in wealth, set aside for your eventual spending needs during retirement. Wow, that was fast! If you are still living at home, driving your dad's hand-me-down hatch-back and eating mom's cooking, it is totally reasonable for you to set aside this kind of dough even if your starting salary is only $36,000 a year (which is $3,000/month or roughly $1,500 per paycheck). Sure, your take-home pay for the year is something like $12,000 but that's still $1,000/month in spending money since you have no "real world" expenses like rent, car payments or food!

If you work at a very small business or if you are self-employed, the IRS also created special retirement vehicles that may allow you to set *even more* aside and makes it easy for you to establish a similar retirement plan. These are variously referred to as Keogh Plans, SIMPLE or SEP-IRAs, which stands for Simplified Employee Pension Individual Retirement Accounts. Again, there are dozens of books written on these topics, but for our purposes, they essentially offer the same opportunities as 401k and 403b plans which apply to most of you.

PORTABILITY

Now, you will probably not stay at the same employer for your entire career. You might be concerned with what happens to all the money in these retirement accounts if you leave, but there's no reason to worry... you can take it with you! If the account balance is more than $5,000, you may be able to leave it in that employer's plan if you really liked the investment options or if the employer had access to specialized funds that you can't find anywhere else. Most new employers will also have their own retirement plan and it is usually a simple matter to instruct your old employer to *rollover* your existing account into the new employer's plan by filling out a pretty simple form. Then you can start at the new employer with a bigger account balance and invest that money in the new fund options available to you. A third route some people choose is to roll the money into a separate investment platform called an *Individual Retirement Account (IRA)* which is available through Fidelity, Vanguard, Charles Schwab, etc.... the same firms that manage employer-sponsored plans since it's the same kind of business for them. A *taxable* IRA is the equivalent of a 401k or 403b – you still owe taxes on that money and will eventually pay when you must take out what is called *Required Minimum Distributions* (RMD) once you turn a certain age. A *non-taxable or Roth IRA* refers to investment funds that have *already* been *taxed* through a special procedure that allows you to *never* pay taxes on the investment gains. The only catch is the maximum amount individuals can contribute any one year is relatively low, like $7,000. But drop that in your compound interest table and play with the return figure... you can grow a tremendous amount of *tax-free* money* this way over the next fifty years of your investing life! Do it!

By the way, *never* "cash out" your retirement plan balance when you do leave one employer for another; instead, roll it over to the new employer or into your IRA account regardless of how big or small the amount. If you accept the distribution and deposit it in your bank account, you will owe taxes on the money and a 10% penalty for "early withdrawal" even if that wasn't what you intended to do. Remember, you want this money invested to grow tax-deferred as long as possible so the balance is as big as possible by the time you are ready to quit working altogether.

In the next chapter, we will explore more practical and realistic scenarios around earning and spending, saving and investing but I really want you to dream about the power of the retirement plan: set aside as much today, including free money from your employers, to earn compounding returns on your investments and have a *huge* balance to support you throughout retirement... a potentially 50 year span of time during which you will probably not want to *work* very hard, but if you save and invest wisely in the meantime, you can *play* really hard!

EXAMPLE ADVICE OF DEPOSIT (PAYCHECK STUB)

Yer Mom	Check Date:	02/01/2019	Emp ID:	6665	Federal:	Married	Work State:	NV	Res. State:	NV
7777 21st Century Blvd	Period:	01/13/2019-01/26/2019	Rate:	200000.00	Allowances:	5	Filing Status:	N/A	Filing Status:	N/A
Hotel, CA 91521	Frequency:	Bi-Week			Additional:	0.00	Allowances:	0	Allowances:	0
	Check/Advice #:	867-5309					Additional:	0.00	Additional:	0.00

HOURS AND EARNINGS / PRE-TAX BENEFITS

		Current		YTD					
Description	Rate	Hours	Earnings	Hours	Earnings	Description	Current	YTD
Regular Salary		72.0	6923.07	176.0	16923.03	401K ($18k/yr)	692.31	2076.93
Float Holiday				16.0	1538.48	FSA DC	192.31	576.93
Holiday	96.16	8.0	769.24	24.0	2307.72	FSA Health Saving	38.47	115.41
Vacation				24.0	2307.70	HSA	161.54	484.62
Group Term Life			16.15		48.45	Medical PreTax	127.05	381.15
HSA Emp Pd			110.00		330.00			
Totals:		80.0	7818.46	240.0	23455.38	Totals:	1211.68	3635.04

TAXES / AFTER-TAX DEDUCTIONS

	Taxable Earnings		Taxes Withheld				
Description	Current	YTD	Current	YTD	Description	Current	YTD
FIT	6496.78	19490.34	829.62	2499.32	Life Ins	9.48	28.44
MEDICARE	7189.09	21567.27	104.25	312.73			
SS	7189.09	21567.27	445.72	1337.17			
NV Misc2	7692.31	23076.93	19.48	58.44			
Totals:			1399.07	4207.66	Totals:	9.48	28.44

	GROSS	less TAXES	less DEDUCTIONS	less IMPUTED INCOME	plus OTHER PYMTS	equals NET PAY
CURRENT	7818.46	1399.07	1221.16	126.15		5072.08
YTD	23455.38	4207.66	3663.48	378.45		15205.79

CURRENT NET PAY DISTRIBUTION AMOUNT / COMPANY INFORMATION / PTO BALANCES ACCRUED YTD AVAILABLE

Dir Dep: Dewey Cheatum N Howe	5072.08	Wheelie Cool Show	Vacation Plan	142.74
Total Current Net Pay:	5072.08	777 Roundabout Way	Float Hol Plan	24.00
		Hotel, CA 91521	Sabbatical Plan	0.00
			Sick Plan	213.20

PRIMARY DEPARTMENT	EMPLOYER MATCH	CURRENT	YTD
Hostess w/ the Mostest	401K ER ($15k max/yr)	576.92	1730.76

MESSAGES Vanna has a crush on Alex Trebek!

CHAPTER 4: SPENDING MONEY

Who doesn't love to spend a little money, right? Honestly, it's the only reason *most* people get a job and then they end up in what's often referred to as the *rat race,* or the *salt mines*, or *keeping up with the Joneses*... none of which sound all that appealing to me, frankly.

The main thing to remember is that you can only spend what you earn, and by earn, of course, we mean have deposited in the bank... your *take home pay* is what is left over after all those taxes and deductions, including retirement money that you *will* get to spend *later*. *Disposable income* is the cash in the bank account that can be used to pay rent or mortgage, gas and insurance for the car, clothes for work, cell phones and subscriptions or food and coffee. Lots of coffee! And ice cream!

INCOME > EXPENSES

Pretty much the simplest expression of inequality for earning and spending money possible, but it's also true. You cannot spend more than you earn. Period. But if you do, you soon end up broke. Bankrupt. Too many people end up in this position because they are financially illiterate; you do not need to be one of them. So, *spend* less than you *earn*...

SPEND < EARN

Right now, most of you do not have *real world expenses* because you are living at home with parents who cover most of your needs like food and clothing and a place to sleep, those are the basics. *Everything* you earn can either go toward spending – not super smart, but unfortunately pretty typical♪ – or saving. Ideally, you should save every penny you can while increasing your earnings.

ASSETS > LIABILITIES = NET WEALTH

If you save consistently, you will end up with *assets*, things that go up in value, and your *net wealth*, or more commonly net worth, will increase. You probably have few if any *liabilities*, which are debts or obligations that decrease your wealth, so anything you save is an increase to your net wealth. Yay! You can further increase your net wealth by adding more assets, saving more, getting returns on investments, or reducing liabilities like paying off debts.

A BALANCED BUDGET LEADS TO A BALANCED LIFE
Creating a *budget* is the best tool for systematically increasing your net wealth. If you can visualize in advance how much you earn and how much you spend, you can usually find a way to save a little (or a lot!) every month and constantly add assets and reduce liabilities. One goal of the financially literate is to increase net wealth to some target by some future date – it helps to "game-ify" a habit-forming lifestyle that results in creating millionaires. For example, when I was kid, probably twelve or thirteen, I decided I wanted to be a millionaire by the time I was 40 years old; no reason, just thought that might be cool. For the next almost 30 years, I played the *game,* it became a habit and now it's *so fun* and *so easy* to save money, invest wisely and acquire assets that go up and up in value! Bottom line: a balanced budget that allows you to spend less than you earn leads to a balanced life that is far more enjoyable and far less stressful than running a rat race or toiling away in a salt mine for the rest of your working life. The budget helps you create good habits and forces you to think about the value of things you buy with your money. It's not bad to spend your money, just make sure the amount you spend and things you buy are in line with your purpose.

BUDGET TEMPLATE

February

Monthly Income	Total monthly	1st half of month	2nd half of month
Semi-Monthly paycheck dates		2/1	2/16
Gross monthly income	$3,600	$1,800	$1,800
Other income	$0	$0	$0
Taxes/deductions ($$)	($900)	($450)	($450)
Retirement deduction ($$)	($100)	($50)	($50)
Total monthly net income	**$2,600**	**$1,300**	**$1,300**
Monthly Expenses			
Tithe, Charity, Giving	($260)	($130)	($130)
Rent/mortgage	($500)		($500)
Electric/gas bill	($40)	($40)	
Utility bill (water/sewer/garbage)	($40)	($40)	
Phone bill	$0		
Cell phone bill	($50)	($50)	
Cable/internet bill	($50)	($50)	
Car insurance bill	($50)	($50)	
Renters/home-owners insurance	$0		
Health insurance (beyond employer coverage)	($100)	($100)	
Life insurance	$0		
Car payment	($200)	($200)	
Credit card bill #1	($50)	($50)	
Credit card bill #2	($100)	($100)	
Credit card bill #3	$0		
Credit card bill #4	$0		
Student debt	$0		
Other expense/debt #1	$0		
Other expense/debt #2	$0		
Total Monthly Expenses	**($1,440)**	**($810)**	**($630)**
Amount left-over after expenses	$1,160	$490	$670
Amount needed for Living Expenses	($800)	($267)	($533)
Amount left to pay off debt/save/invest	$360	$223	$137

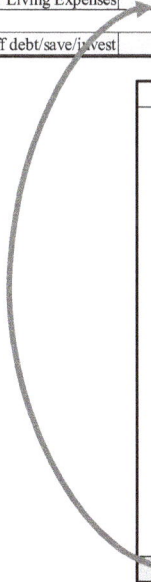

Living Expenses Tally	
$300	groceries
$100	gas / parking
$50	clothes
$200	coffee & restaurants
$20	gifts
$20	haircuts/beauty
$50	dates
$0	?
$0	?
$0	?
$0	?
$0	?
$0	?
$0	?
$0	?
$0	?
$0	?
$60	misc.
$800	$$ needed to live on

39

This is a simplified personal budget template⸱. The appendix at the end of this book goes into far more detail, but this will get us started thinking about what a budget does and how it helps. It is an intuitive way to visualize the money you earn and the money you spend, both spread across two pay periods per month. My preferred method is to look at this on a monthly basis, but when I first got started in a career, I built one of these templates for each bi-weekly paycheck (every two weeks). The only small difference between twice a month and every two weeks happens twice a year when you get *an extra paycheck* for the month – because there are four and a half weeks every month, so every six months, there's an extra two-week pay period. It's just math, yo. Well, that and a Gregorian calendar, I guess. But who really gets paid on a lunar cycle? Argh, so hard to focus when someone says *budget*!

The budget is a living document, meaning it should be updated as life changes, whether on the income side or the expense side. You get a new job, update the top as soon as you figure out how the gross and net and deductions are all affected; have a side gig, add that in or take it out if you stop doing it. Add a new monthly subscription or update your monthly phone bill as things change; landlord raised your rent, update the figure; started going to church or pledged a monthly charity amount, drop it right in. This is a flexible template that will accommodate your changing financial life for about ten years; by then you should be savvy enough to build your own.

KNOWN OR FIXED EXPENSES

Gross income gets reduced by taxes and deductions but maybe you have a side gig that generates *other income*, too. All that goes into your Net Income. Then you have known, fixed expenses for things like rent or a mortgage or maybe a car payment and car insurance. These are amounts that are known in advance, scheduled, for a specific period of time. Those are easy to put down and plan to cover each month; they are also probably the biggest expenses each month.

Utility bills and things like cell phone contracts are fairly well known, typical and constantly changing by only small amounts. Usually, we just average the last six months or a years' worth of monthly bills and use that as an estimate for budgeting purposes.

VARIABLE LIVING EXPENSES

Then there are things we buy often but the amount we spend on them varies – sometimes wildly – from month to month. Call these *living expenses*: things like groceries, gas and parking, clothes and shoes, cosmetics, coffee and going out to eat with friends, gifts... ever go on a date that was free? Lucky you. Some of these things we can control, others we just gotta do to stay in the game. So maybe now is a good time to mention *needs* versus *wants*.

SHELTER AND HYGIENE

As mentioned earlier, the basic needs are: food, shelter, clothing. Prioritize your spending so you never find yourself without these *basic necessities*. Shelter, or a home, can be an apartment, condo, house or a room in your parent's basement or attic. It should be warm in winter and sufferable during summer, generally free of pests (siblings), fumes, or water leaks. Most importantly, it should have a toilet, shower and sink... maybe a kitchen would be nice. You get the idea. You don't have to fill up the space with *things*, but most of us do. And some things are helpful, may even become necessary (Coffee machine! Fridge for ice cream!) but be thoughtful about it rather than just try to keep up with the Joneses. Shelter leads to good hygiene which allows you to get a job and make more money. Staying with family or friends is usually a low-budget way to accumulate wealth faster compared to taking on a high-rent obligation in the hip part of town just to feel cool. How cool is it to own your home and a few rentals by the time you're 30 versus paying the landlord more than half your salary every month to live with a roommate in that 500 square feet garage apartment with a 90210-zip code'? Yeah, thought so. You're sooooo cool.

FOOD AND SECURITY

Food is security; without it we tend not to perform very well or for very long. Most Americans do not suffer a shortage of food, maybe a shortage of wise food choices, but no shortage of calories. Instead, we tend to waste a lot of money on eating out, or eating conveniently and we generally make poor nutritional decisions. Groceries are cheaper than a sit-down restaurant, takeout or delivery. Junk food is called junk for a reason, hello! As you watch your spending on food, think about the different kinds of value you get out of a steak dinner, sushi, Taco Bell or homemade soup and salad with ham and cheese on rye: there's monetary value, nutritional value and social value, probably others, but you have to be thoughtful, achieve nutrition and weigh the amount of time and money it takes for each meal. Going out to eat lunch every day at the office is *way* more expensive than making a sandwich and eating some chopped veggies at your desk. How much of a sacrifice is that to accomplish your financial goals and stay within your budget? Also, you might live longer.

CLOTHING AND CONFIDENCE

Clothes are another necessity that Madison Avenue has turned into a pursuit of desire. If you are naked or sloppily dressed or never have clean clothes, chances are you will not hold down that job for long. Great paying jobs are often customer-facing and the impression you make usually determines how much that client will spend with you. Clothes can build confidence and can help you fit in with your peers, but clothes seldom require outrageous spending – you put that pressure on yourself because advertisers are successfully trying to separate you from your money. Consider how much you spend on a pair of shoes or a handbag or business suit and figure out how much money that item helped you earn; make sure it was a profitable purchase. Alternatively, think about that item's cost divided by the number of times you wore it or used it. Again, make a game of spending as little as possible but getting the most value out of anything you buy. Find a happy threshold like $1 per time you wore those jeans (50 times for a $50 pair of jeans) or $5 per day you wore those fancy shoes (100 days for $500 shoes) and tell yourself you won't buy any more of whatever it is until you get that much value from the ones you already own. Don't be ridiculous here but find a way to measure and evaluate whether the stuff you spend your money on is really worth it! How much closer did those items help you get to accomplishing your purpose?

NEEDS VERSUS WANTS

When you are planning out your monthly living expenses, keep these ideas in mind: Spend what you *must* spend on needs and try to *minimize* the amount you spend on wants. Netflix and Spotify are *wants*; the cell phone is probably a *need* but how many apps require monthly subscriptions and are those needs or wants? Don't be stingy with gifts but be thoughtful about them and maybe get crafty and make your own or plan to do something fun but free together with friends instead of giving things that likely get thrown away in a month. As many of your peers get married, there may be some expensive gifts or destination travel required so be sure and plan for those things.

GOOD HABITS: MONTHLY, WEEKLY, DAILY

At the end of each month, it is good practice to pull out all the receipts from things you bought and add up everything, create new categories if you need to and track it all. If you don't measure what you're spending, you cannot manage what you're spending. At the end of *every* month, I invariably ask myself "why in the world did I feel the need to buy that?" and regret that I no longer have that money to save or spend on something I'd rather have. Habitually reviewing your expenditures *every month* will hone your ability to choose more wisely and eventually you will spend less on wasteful things; instead, you will find more left over in your bank account and have more to invest.

Maybe don't just wait until the *end* of each month, practice your mental accounting at the end of each pay period or every week. How closely did you match your budgeted expectation? Do you recall spending that extra $4 for a soda while out at lunch with your office colleagues? Could've been free water! Starbucks six times this week instead of only the three you budgeted? It is hard to make good habits, but it is even *harder* to break bad habits! Make good spending habits now while you're still young and it will accrue to your net wealth for many more decades.

Personally, I've broken everything I spend down to a daily amount and I think about it every day, usually less than a minute because it is such an ingrained habit by now, but I can tell you whether I'm on track or ahead or behind pretty much any day of the week. There are few surprises in my budget life, but when there *are* surprises, I have plenty of savings already set aside to handle them, so it doesn't blow a hole in my budget or force me to take on debt. You will have a few surprises, too, and you will be able to cover unexpected expenses with cash savings if you make this chapter central to your life.

REACTING VERSUS PLANNING

It takes perfect practice to be perfect, but in this case, you only need a plan and some good habits. Good habits allow you to execute tasks without a lot of psychic energy, so things feel like they just happen. When you go through the initial burden of thinking through where your money is spent, it forces you to evaluate and weigh whether those expenditures were or will continue to be worth the time and energy it took you to earn that much money. With that in mind, you can project forward, or *forecast*, how much money you need to earn to continue that lifestyle or even to upgrade to a "better" lifestyle, however you define that. Soon you can begin thinking in terms of weeks, months or even years forward. If you can think *that* far ahead, you can figure out how much money you need to make today, save today and invest today so that you have resources to draw from in the future. We call the short-term, *backward-looking* approach *reacting*: you already spent money on certain things, and you can't really control near-term obligations like utilities or contracted payments. The longer-term, *forward-looking* approach we call *planning*: you can survive without buying these things or signing up for those services and instead save up for some big expense like a car repair or vacation if you can imagine and plan for that big expense coming.

Americans have so many *things* competing for their money and that is driven by advertisers and marketing. Businesses are created to sell you something even if you don't *need* it, but they have learned how to get you to *want* it enough to command a portion of your wallet. Since a dollar can only be spent on one thing, you must be thoughtful enough to slow down the purchase impulse and evaluate the long-term cost of buying *anything* beyond necessities. Do you really need that 26th pair of shoes? Will that 120th video game or movie really get averaged down to $0.25 per play? Can you really listen to one million songs on that music app or listen to the fifty songs you really love enough to turn $12 *per month* into a good value? If you order a DoorDash meal from your favorite restaurant, aren't you still going to be as hungry for the next meal as if you made yourself a burrito at home? Convenience is costly and service isn't free; serve yourself and pay yourself a generous tip!

CASH IS KING

Businesses have made it extremely *easy* and *thoughtless* to spend your money. People used to get paid in cash or with a check that had to be deposited into a bank account. Then people had to pull out their cash whenever they bought something, seeing every hard-earned dollar get handed over while their pile of dollar bills got smaller and smaller. It was a physical act, visual, tangible and impossible to ignore, so every time we spent money, we felt it! And it hurt!

CREDIT CARDS FOR THE MASSES

Then came along credit cards, this little plastic square that magically covered the cost of a meal or clothes or gas at the pump. No fuss, maybe a signature... but then they gave you the card back, so all's well! Didn't lose a thing in the moment and you didn't have to pay it off until the end of the month!   When folks needed more encouragement to spend, the card companies introduced points and cash-back and miles, anything to make you feel like you "earned" something in exchange for spending money on whatever you wanted to buy. If you got distracted into building a big points balance, or "earning" enough miles for a "free" flight, you ignored how much you spent – marketers created a game of mental accounting in which they win more of *your* money in *their* pockets.

Then at the end of every month after what is called a *grace period*, you got a bill that said you only had to pay a fraction – usually something like 3% or 5% – of the total amount you actually spent that month! What a deal: you spent $100 dollars this month but only had to pay $5! Except, if you paid only that minimum amount, your bill would get bigger the next month even if you didn't buy anything else. Wait, how is that possible? I didn't buy anything this month, I paid $5 for $100 worth of purchases the prior month... why is my new bill $96.90? We will cover *interest expense* shortly, but that $1.90 *finance charge* is an insidious cancer that will eat away at your hard-earned money if you use it irresponsibly. Many people in my generation didn't understand – they were financially illiterate; most people *still today* only face up to it once it is too late to easily recover.

Debit cards are just as easy to use for spending, but the money at least comes out of your bank account, so you're just reducing your own asset rather than increasing a liability; still, your net wealth is decreasing with each purchase. You are smart enough to look at your bank account balance at the end of each month and realize how small that balance is compared to what you thought you earned. Start asking yourself how to keep more of the money you earn!

Today, transactions can happen as fast as your phone recognizes your face or thumb, sometimes even faster! CashApp, Venmo and ApplePay have evolved to make spending super easy, even if you don't have money in the bank. Autopay features reduce the pain of seeing that bill every month because the money just automatically leaves your bank account or gets charged to your card or ApplePay balance without any effort on your part. Yes, this is convenient and might reduce the amount of late fees you used to pay, but you probably never realize or think about how much you are spending and where all that money is going. At least one business has even created an app to look through your autopay amounts to ask you if you even use those services anymore!

STICK WITH THE PLAN

A lazy mind is a poor soul. Since you want to be financially literate, you need to develop a habit, a knee-jerk reaction, an instinct like spitting out bitter or flinching from anything fast-moving near your head... when it comes to spending money, pause for a moment and ask if this is in your plan, your budget, and if it is an expense worth the money you earned. You should also be thinking about how to increase your earnings and investment returns, keeping more of what you earn by reducing taxes, but the biggest benefit you can gain for yourself is to stop spending. Work back to prioritize necessities (shelter, food, clothing) and then be thoughtful about every other dollar you spend with an idea of how much value it will provide. That eighth coffee cup with a witty slogan along with that cute, tasseled pillow for the couch nobody is allowed to sit on... will *not* help you achieve your purpose or meet your financial goals, and the brief tickle of joy those things give you will *evaporate* before you even get the credit card bill! In a later chapter you will see how the math works but take that $50 you just spent on a coffee mug and throw(away) pillow and pretend you instead invested it at a 5% annual return. In 50 years, when you're retired, that $50 would be worth more than $600. That's *at least* one doctor's visit (which you will probably need by then)!

Here's another back-to-the-future moment: in 50 years, when you can no longer work because you are too old, either physically or mentally or just too darn cantankerous to put up with other people, your living expenses will likely be higher for insurance, medicine, travel or even things like assisted living, walkers and canes. Insurance will probably be your biggest expense, even if you rely on Medicare since that is just basic coverage. Dental care – think dentures – isn't cheap and isn't covered except through supplemental insurance. At some point, you will probably move out of your condo or house in the suburbs because you will need help remembering when to take your medicine, whether you already took your medicine and where you last left your pants'. No, the clean ones. Well, it looks like you need help with laundry now, too. Home health care is expensive!

Yes, all of this is a bit fanciful and way, way far in the future, but funny thing about the future: it tends to catch up with you more quickly than you think it will! If you've spent any time thinking about, dreaming about what you want to do with your life, what your purpose is in life, then you need to draft a plan that will help you achieve that aspirational goal rather than maintain a fleeting lifestyle. Remember, money isn't the goal, it's just a tool to help you achieve whatever your goal is. *That's* why you need to create a budget – it is the best tool for maximizing one of the most important tools, *money*, to fulfill your purpose. Debt makes financial goals harder to achieve; keeping your income greater than your expenses will steer you away from debt. The budget will help you stick with the plan by making your income greater than expenses by enough to pay for that (potentially *very* expensive) future. The good news is that once you've gone through the work of creating and living with a budget for a while, it becomes a deeply ingrained *good* habit and since habits are hard to break, living within a budget and making wise money choices will become as easy as putting on your pants... just as soon as you find them.

The following four pages are snapshots of the template Budget Input and Budget Output worksheets included with the purchase of this book. The QR code below links to an Excel file for your download and use. Additional instructions for modifying this budget template to suit your own lifestyle are provided in Appendix A.

BUDGET TEMPLATE

...AND FOR YOUR CONSIDERATION

Monthly Income	February		
	Total monthly	1st half of month	2nd half of month
Semi-Monthly paycheck dates		2/1	2/16
Gross monthly income	$3,600	$1,800	$1,800
Other income	$0	$0	$0
Taxes/deductions ($$)	($900)	($450)	($450)
Retirement deduction ($$)	($100)	($50)	($50)
Total monthly net income	$2,600	$1,300	$1,300
Monthly Expenses			
Tithe, Charity, Giving	($260)	($130)	($130)
Rent/mortgage	($500)		($500)
Electric/gas bill	($40)	($40)	
Utility bill (water/sewer/garbage)	($40)	($40)	
Phone bill	$0		
Cell phone bill	($50)	($50)	
Cable/internet bill	($50)	($50)	
Car insurance bill	($50)	($50)	
Renters/home-owners insurance	$0		
Health insurance (beyond employer coverage)	($100)	($100)	
Life insurance	$0		
Car payment	($200)	($200)	
Credit card bill #1	($50)	($50)	
Credit card bill #2	($100)	($100)	
Credit card bill #3	$0		
Credit card bill #4	$0		
Student debt	$0		
Other expense/debt #1	$0		
Other expense/debt #2	$0		
Total Monthly Expenses	($1,440)	($810)	($630)
Amount left-over after expenses	$1,160	$490	$670
Amount needed for Living Expenses	($800)	($267)	($533)

Got a side gig? Royalties from songs or movie credits? Tips and garage sale proceeds probably go here, too.
Adjust this based on your paystubs or actual from last year. FICA/SSI/State/Medicare/Medical-Dental
If co. matches a 401(k), 403(b) contribution, make at least the minimum to get the match - free money!

Currently set to 10%, but adjust as appropriate.
Show in the last half of each month to ensure its available by the first of the next month.
Average the last 12 months of bills; summer is more expensive if a/c runs all the time!
Again, average over the last year. Maybe don't water the lawn or take shorter showers?
Or maybe it's monthly app subscriptions now - anyone a gamer?

Add up Netflix, Prime, Hulu or whatever - no cheating!
You can set for pmt in first half or second half of the month; try to balance across each paycheck.
Usually required by landlord or mortgage company. Shop around for the best deal!
Might come out of your paycheck above, or maybe parents cover it?
Usually not necessary until you have a family and significant financial obligations.
Always pay the minimum required; never be late; pay extra when able
Always pay the minimum required; never be late; pay extra when able
Always pay the minimum required; never be late; pay extra when able

50

BUDGET TEMPLATE (CONTINUED)

...MAKE A TARGET OR GOAL, ENJOY THE GAME!

Debt totals:	Total owed	Interest rate	Min. payment
Car	$5,000	6.0%	$200
Credit card bill #1	$1,500	12.0%	$50
Credit card bill #2	$2,000	18.0%	$45
Credit card bill #3	$0	0.0%	
Credit card bill #4	$0	0.0%	
Student debt	$0	0.0%	
Other expense/debt #1	$0	0.0%	
Other expense/debt #2	$0	0.0%	

Asset totals:		
Liquid assets:	Total accrued	Interest rate
Checking Accounts	$2,200	1.0%
Savings Accounts	$1,000	1.0%
Brokerage Accounts/Mutual Funds/ETF's	$0	
Stock Options	$0	

Non-liquid assets:	Current Value	Yield
Employer Retirement Account	$2,500	1.0%
Regular IRA	$0	
Roth IRA	$1,500	1.0%
CD/Time Deposits (Maturity Date)	$500	2.0%
Insurance Cash Value	$0	
Investment Property #1	$0	
Note to Borrower #1	$0	9.0%

Living Expenses Tally	
$300 groceries	$10/day. Adjust as needed; compare to previous month… every month
$100 gas / parking	If not gas, then probably a similar amount for an Uber or bus.
$50 clothes	Great gift requests, especially dress clothes for work.
$200 coffee & restaurants	$7/day? Minimize this if you can, but keep track of it every time you go out.
$20 gifts	Usually impossible to avoid these - put something aside in case.
$20 haircuts/beauty	Usually impossible to avoid these - put something aside in case.
$50 dates	Not bad to plan for good times and show her/him it's in the budget.
$0 ?	
$0 ?	
$0 ?	
$0 ?	
$0 ?	
$0 ?	
$0 ?	
$60 misc.	
$800 $$ needed to live on	

Budget for [year 2024]

CASH FLOW STATEMENT

Month	February	March	April	May	June	July	August	September	October	November	December	January
Payday	2/1/24	3/1/24	4/1/24	5/1/24	6/1/24	7/1/24	8/1/24	9/1/24	10/15/24	11/1/24	12/1/24	1/1/25
Semi-monthly net income	$1,300	$1,300	$1,300	$1,300	$1,300	$1,300	$1,300	$1,300	$1,300	$1,300	$1,300	$1,300
Tithe, Charity, Giving	($130)	($130)	($130)	($130)	($130)	($130)	($130)	($130)	($130)	($130)	($130)	($130)
Rent/mortgage												
Electric/gas bill	($40)	($40)	($40)	($40)	($40)	($40)	($40)	($40)	($40)	($40)	($40)	($40)
Utility bill (water/sewer/garbage)	($40)	($40)	($40)	($40)	($40)	($40)	($40)	($40)	($40)	($40)	($40)	($40)
Phone bill												
Cell phone bill	($50)	($50)	($50)	($50)	($50)	($50)	($50)	($50)	($50)	($50)	($50)	($50)
Cable/internet bill	($50)	($50)	($50)	($50)	($50)	($50)	($50)	($50)	($50)	($50)	($50)	($50)
Car insurance bill	($50)	($50)	($50)	($50)	($50)	($50)	($50)	($50)	($50)	($50)	($50)	($50)
Renters/home-owners insurance												
Health insurance (beyond employer coverage)	($100)	($100)	($100)	($100)	($100)	($100)	($100)	($100)	($100)	($100)	($100)	($100)
Life insurance												
Car payment	($200)	($200)	($200)	($200)	($200)	($200)	($200)	($200)	($200)	($200)	($200)	($200)
Credit card bill #1	($50)	($50)	($50)	($50)	($50)	($50)	($50)	($50)	($50)	($50)	($50)	($50)
Credit card bill #2	($100)	($100)	($100)	($100)	($100)	($100)	($100)	($100)	($100)	($100)	($100)	($100)
Credit card bill #3												
Credit card bill #4												
Student debt												
Other expense/debt #1												
Other expense/debt #2												
Savings	($223)	($223)	($223)	($223)	($223)	($223)	($223)	($223)	($223)	($223)	($223)	($223)
Other Unbudgeted Expenses Actually Incurred												
Total for living	$267	$267	$267	$267	$267	$267	$267	$267	$267	$267	$267	$267

Payday	2/15/24	3/15/24	4/15/24	5/15/24	6/15/24	7/15/24	8/15/24	9/15/24	10/15/24	11/15/24	12/15/24	1/15/25
Semi-monthly net income	$1,300	$1,300	$1,300	$1,300	$1,300	$1,300	$1,300	$1,300	$1,300	$1,300	$1,300	$1,300
Tithe, Charity, Giving	($130)	($130)	($130)	($130)	($130)	($130)	($130)	($130)	($130)	($130)	($130)	($130)
Rent/mortgage	($500)	($500)	($500)	($500)	($500)	($500)	($500)	($500)	($500)	($500)	($500)	($500)
Electric/gas bill												
Utility bill (water/sewer/garbage)												
Phone bill												
Cell phone bill												
Cable/internet bill												
Car insurance bill												
Renters/home-owners insurance												
Health insurance (beyond employer coverage)												
Life insurance												
Car payment												
Credit card bill #1												
Credit card bill #2												
Credit card bill #3												
Credit card bill #4												
Student debt												
Other expense/debt #1												
Other expense/debt #2												
Savings	($137)	($137)	($137)	($137)	($137)	($137)	($137)	($137)	($137)	($137)	($137)	($137)
Other Unbudgeted Expenses Actually Incurred												
Total for living	$533	$533	$533	$533	$533	$533	$533	$533	$533	$533	$533	$533

See what happens if you have an unexpected expense of $800 this month. What if it was only $200?

BALANCE SHEET

Debts	Beginning Balance													Ending Balance
Car payment	$5,000	$4,825	$4,649	$4,472	$4,295	$4,116	$3,937	$3,756	$3,575	$3,393	$3,210	$3,026	$2,841	$2,841
Credit card bill #1	$1,500	$1,465	$1,430	$1,394	$1,358	$1,321	$1,285	$1,248	$1,210	$1,172	$1,134	$1,095	$1,056	$1,056
Credit card bill #2	$2,000	$1,930	$1,859	$1,787	$1,714	$1,639	$1,564	$1,487	$1,410	$1,331	$1,251	$1,170	$1,087	$1,087
Credit card bill #3														
Credit card bill #4														
Student debt														
Other expense/debt #1														
Other expense/debt #2														
Total debt	$8,500	$8,220	$7,938	$7,653	$7,366	$7,077	$6,785	$6,491	$6,195	$5,896	$5,595	$5,291	$4,985	$4,985

Assets	Beginning Balance													Ending Balance
Monthly savings		$360	$360	$360	$360	$360	$360	$360	$360	$360	$360	$360	$360	$360
Checking Accounts	$2,200	$2,462	$2,724	$2,880	$2,880	$2,880	$2,880	$2,880	$2,880	$2,880	$2,880	$2,880	$2,880	$2,880
Savings Accounts	$1,000	$1,001	$1,002	$1,106	$1,367	$1,628	$1,890	$2,151	$2,413	$2,675	$2,880	$2,880	$2,880	$2,880
Brokerage Accounts/Mutual Funds/ETFs										$55	$260	$260	$260	$260
Stock Options														
Liquid subtotal	$3,200	$3,463	$3,726	$3,986	$4,247	$4,508	$4,770	$5,031	$5,293	$5,555	$5,815	$6,020	$6,020	$6,020
Employer Retirement Account	$2,500	$2,600	$2,700	$2,800	$2,900	$3,000	$3,100	$3,200	$3,300	$3,400	$3,500	$3,600	$3,700	$3,700
Regular IRA														
Roth IRA	$1,500	$100	$100	$100	$100	$100	$100	$100	$100	$100	$100	$100	$100	$100
Non-liquid subtotal	$4,000	$2,700	$2,800	$2,900	$3,000	$3,100	$3,200	$3,300	$3,400	$3,500	$3,600	$3,700	$3,800	$3,800
Total assets	$7,200	$6,163	$6,526	$6,886	$7,247	$7,608	$7,970	$8,331	$8,693	$9,055	$9,415	$9,720	$9,820	$12,420

Extra Paycheck #1
$1,300 Net Income
($130) Tithe, Charity, Giving
$1,170 Total (to pay down debt or invest)

Extra Paycheck #2
$1,300 Net Income
($130) Tithe, Charity, Giving
$1,170 Total (to pay down debt or invest)

CHAPTER 5: DEBT

Compound interest on debt was the banker's greatest invention, to capture and enslave a productive society.

- Albert Einstein

When super smart people warn against debt, maybe we should pay attention. The truth is, though, that most people in the U.S. have "accumulated" some amount of debt. The most common kinds of debt are things like credit card balances, car loans, home loans, student loans. Almost every business carries some kind of debt and oftentimes a whole heaping gob of it! Our government has borrowed so much from other countries and individuals that it would take more than a year's worth of *all* our economic productivity to pay the debt off. So, debt is a commonplace thing, but why?

Because somewhere along the way **income < expenses** for too long and in order to "balance the books" money was borrowed from someone who had savings to invest. Notice the inequality in that last sentence is *backwards*, meaning income *was less than* expenses rather than what the fundamental inequality requires, that income *should <u>always</u> be more than* expenses. Part of the problem is our sense of *want it right now*! Few people have saved enough of their earnings to pay for everything they may spontaneously want to buy. Financially literate people learn to delay spending money they do not have so they do not have to incur that dangerous beast called DEBT.

COSTLY ADVANCE ON FUTURE EARNINGS

Debt is an obligation you assume, or incur, as an advance and a *burden* against your future earnings. Just because a business will sell you something they have *on credit* does not mean it is free. In fact, it will turn out to be much more expensive over time! So, let's walk through an example, see how debt works, how much it costs and why it should be avoided by most people in most cases.

PRINCIPAL

You figure you'll need a new laptop once you graduate from school, so you shop around and find one that meets your needs – maybe not everything you want, of course, because you read this book – and discover it costs $2,400, all taxes and software included. You don't have that much saved yet, but you were just offered a credit card from your bank or from an airline that promised you 40,000 miles just for signing up, or from the merchant who wants to sell you the laptop – bam! you have a $2,500 spending limit. No problem then... *swipe!* And now you owe $2,400 to Visa or Mastercard or whatever. The merchant who sold you the computer has to pay the credit card company a 2%-4% *service fee* on the purchase price amount, but they get to keep the rest of your $2,400 to cover sales tax, *their* costs and a profit. The balance you owe, called the principal amount, is $2,400 and if you paid off that card at the end of the *grace period* – which is the time between your purchase and the credit card bill *due date* – then that's all you'd have to pay. Huh, why would the credit card pay the merchant and collect payment from you 20-50 days later for just 2%-4%? Do it enough times – U.S. retail sales in 2023 were roughly $600 billion per month, so $7.2 trillion for the year! – and that 2%-4% really adds up (to $217 billion)! But not everyone uses a credit card and not all sales are final, etc. etc.

INTEREST

The *real* reason card companies insert themselves in the middle of transactions is for the opportunity to collect *finance charges* from you. That is an interest rate that is charged on the *debt balance,* the amount you charged and have not yet paid back. Here's the real sticker shock for you: the interest rates are usually in the range of 18% to 24% *per year*. So, if you carried the full purchase price balance for a whole year, you would pay another, let's say, 20% of the purchase price, one-fifth of the original cost! The card companies only encourage you to pay the minimum amount, something like 5% of the outstanding balance every month, so they can earn interest on a bigger balance for a longer time period. *Anyone* carrying a balance on credit card terms is *foolish* with their money, spending far more than the list price for the things they buy; they are not financially literate.

Do not fall into this trap; pay off the full balance of any charges before the due date.

TERM

The next example is a car loan which differs slightly from the credit card example above in which the interest rate varies or *floats* over time (but it's *always* really high) and the amount you have to pay each month also varies over time. The lender on a car loan wants to get paid back before the car is worthless so they extend the loan only for a *fixed term* or time. Also, they have *security*: if you fail to pay them back, they can take the car and resell it to recover *part* of what they lent you. The result of all this is a fixed term and fixed payment for a lower interest rate loan.

For example, you have your eye on a *sweeeet* Chrysler 300, for whatever reason, but the salesman says he can't go lower than $25,000 tax, title, license and floor mats included, an amount, of course, you don't have *already saved* in your bank account even though your budget *is* balanced with income more than expenses. But don't worry says the salesman, they will lend you the money to buy the car today by paying $2,500 now and then over the next five years by paying *only* $500 per month. Hey! You have $500 per month in extra earnings and some expenses that you can cut back on, so *let's goooo!*

The figure on the following page is an *amortization table* which illustrates the month-by-month accrual of interest, progress of monthly principal and interest (P/I) payments, and the slowly declining balance of borrowed money that is being repaid. This is the shortened version of the full schedule available in the Excel file for you to download and use. Amortization is just the process of paying off a debt, including interest, with a fixed payment amount over the term of the loan.

Five Year Car Loan for $22,500 at 12% Interest

			BALANCE	INTEREST 12.00%	P/I PMT	BALANCE
						22,500
Jan	2025	1	22,500	225	500.00	22,225
Feb		2	22,225	222	500	21,947
Mar		3	21,947	219	500	21,667
Apr		4	21,667	217	500	21,383
May		5	21,383	214	500	21,097
Jun		6	21,097	211	500	20,808
Jul		7	20,808	208	500	20,516
Aug		8	20,516	205	500	20,221
Sep		9	20,221	202	500	19,924
Oct		10	19,924	199	500	19,623
Nov		11	19,623	196	500	19,319
Dec		12	19,319	193	500	19,012
Jan	2026	13	19,012	190	500	18,702
Feb		14	18,702	187	500	18,389
...	...	...	...	...	...	...
Oct	2030	58	1,510	15	500	1,025
Nov		59	1,025	10	500	535
Dec		60	535.49	5.35	540.84	-
			TOTAL:	7,541	30,041	

Well, congratulations, I guess. You just bought a $25,000 car for $32,541 ($30,041 in principal and interest payments, plus the initial $2,500 down payment). Oh, and you had to carry – for five years – the super expensive kind of insurance called *comprehensive collision coverage* since the lender doesn't want to risk you having an accident and sticking them with a car that's worth less than they lent you. Yikes, sure hope you got a lot of valuable use out of that car which is probably only worth $12,500 now... max.

Let's see how that worked out. The balance in the first month is exactly what was borrowed, $22,500. The interest rate is 12% per year, so 1% per month. Multiply the monthly interest rate times the balance at the end of the prior month to get $225. Then the payment of $500 comes in to pay – *first!* – the interest and *then* whatever remains is applied to the principal balance. If you are late any one month, *that* fee is paid out of your payment first, then interest, then principal. But you are almost financially literate, so you at least make all your payments on time; after your first $500 monthly payment you now owe $22,225. That pattern repeats itself until you get to the last month, when you owe $535.49, and your interest cost comes in at $5.35 so you write a check for the extra $40.84 to just be done with it all. *Whew*! Too stressful – get a hot rod Lincoln' instead... sheesh.

Why not just lease the car instead of buying one with debt? OK, let's debunk this myth in a hurry. A lease is just another way of saying rent: an "obligation to pay" for "a period of time" at the end of which you surrender, or return, the asset. At the beginning of a car lease, you pay a little money up front, something like 5% to 10% of the car's current value. Then, you make monthly payments, just like with debt, until your lease term expires, usually three years, or 36 months, sometimes longer or shorter. During those three years you still must maintain the car, get oil changes, tune-ups and fill it up with gas or electricity, and carry expensive insurance coverage. At the end of the lease period, they check if you stayed within your mileage allowance, which is a limit on the number of miles you are allowed to put on the vehicle – *each* mile over that limit costs you an exorbitant amount, like $0.10 or $0.25 *per mile* – because miles driven reduces the resale value of the vehicle. Why does that matter? Because you don't own the car, the car company that leased it to you still owns it! They get the car back at the end of the lease and you have nothing to show for three years of payments except a big hole in your bank account! All those monthly payments should have been going to acquire assets, but you just paid rent for a vehicle! The car will be worth less than it was originally worth, but probably didn't fall in value as much as your payments totaled: let's say you paid $350/month for 36 months after paying $1,500 upfront for a $25,000 car... so, that's $14,100 in payments. If the car is still worth $12,500, the car owner can resell it – maybe for more than that – or lease it again or finance a new borrower and make even more! If you purchase the car outright, you can drive it as many miles as you want, until it either falls apart or you sell it. Any car has some residual value, and just like renting a house, if you lease a car, you don't own that residual value, you're just paying someone to use their asset! Don't be fooled by "paying less per month" since you do not end up owning anything once the payments are finished, whereas you *do* own an asset after paying off a car loan... even if it is worth much less than the original purchase price.

Better still, save the same amount of money as the car payment or lease would be each month. *Compound* the interest it earns so you can buy your cars with cash!

GOOD DEBT

All kidding aside, debt is expensive and stressful and the decision to assume debt should be considered thoroughly. That said, there are potentially good reasons to have debt in cases where the asset you are acquiring is likely to go up in value over the time the debt is outstanding: a single-family house and cash-flowing investment properties are the standard examples here. Another example of good debt: you may be able to borrow money at a lower cost than the return that can be earned investing that money in very safe investments with a similar time horizon to retiring the debt, also called *maturity*.

I am a big fan of education and the acquisition of knowledge – an asset that offers a lifetime of returns! If you must borrow money to attend post-secondary education, you should evaluate the potential for your eventual job(s) or career(s) to generate enough earnings to repay that debt *in addition to* supporting the lifestyle you budget for yourself. Reread that last sentence a few times and do some math, use an amortization table. No kidding, do it! Don't count on your lender or the government to forgive your student debt, ethics considerations aside, and make sure you are willing to lower your lifestyle to cover the costs of any debt you incur. The interest expense – as well as the principal repayment – *must* be part of your budget, eating up dollars that could otherwise be spent on other things or else saved and invested for when you can't work.

HOME MORTGAGE EXAMPLE

Since it might be a kind of good debt, let's explore what it means to have a home *mortgage*. You've all seen or heard your parents stressing over the mortgage payment – but what does that mean? Most people cannot buy a house with just their cash savings, it is such a big dollar amount compared to what most people earn in wages. There is a huge, well-funded and smoothly operating mortgage market that makes it relatively easy to buy a house using borrowed money. Banks and mortgage brokers are the largest *underwriters* and there are dozens of online businesses interested in your mortgage application: it's a big money business! Open the amortization table tab in the Excel file – same one used for the car loan – and adjust the figures for buying a $250,000 house with a 30-year, 6% fixed rate, 80% loan-to-value mortgage. That means you are taking out a $200,000 loan (80% of $250,000) with a 6% annual interest rate and you will pay that loan off in fixed payments over the next 30 years. (No wonder our parents were so stressed, that's a lot of expensive money over a really long time!) Just like the car loan example, the first month's interest is calculated as 6% divided by 12 months, times the original loan balance of $200,000. I made the numbers up so the math would be easy. Interest expense for the first month is $1,000 and your payments for the next 360 months are set at $1,200. So, after your first monthly payment you only knocked off $200 of your $200,000 mortgage and the lender made $1,000 of interest income. Over the life of this loan, unless you pay it off sooner, you will pay almost $231,100 in *interest*, in addition to the $200,000 you borrowed. If you live in a city or area where housing prices go up by roughly 6% annually, you made out OK, not great, but you didn't *lose* any money on the investment – and you got to live in it that whole time. Of course, you might have since moved out and turned it into a rental, letting others pay that mortgage for you, in which case it was a wise investment even though you took on debt to get it.

Thirty Year $200,000 Home Mortgage at 6%

			BALANCE	INTEREST 6.00%	P/I PMT	BALANCE
						200,000
Jan	2025	1	200,000	1,000	1,200.00	199,800
Feb		2	199,800	999	1,200	199,599
Mar		3	199,599	998	1,200	199,397
Apr		4	199,397	997	1,200	199,194
May		5	199,194	996	1,200	198,990
Jun		6	198,990	995	1,200	198,785
Jul		7	198,785	994	1,200	198,579
Aug		8	198,579	993	1,200	198,372
Sep		9	198,372	992	1,200	198,164
Oct		10	198,164	991	1,200	197,954
Nov		11	197,954	990	1,200	197,744
Dec		12	197,744	989	1,200	197,533
Jan	2026	13	197,533	988	1,200	197,321
...	...	...	...	...	...	...
Dec	2029	60	186,314	932	1,200	186,046
...	...	...	...	...	...	...
Dec	2034	120	167,586	838	1,200	167,224
...	...	...	...	...	...	...
Dec	2039	180	142,325	712	1,200	141,836
...	...	...	...	...	...	...
Dec	2054	360	296	1	297	-
			TOTAL:	231,097	431,097	

BAD DEBT

Unfortunately, most people are on the wrong side of debt. They use it to buy *wants* and luxuries – like new furniture or fancy clothes or vacations or jewelry – and liabilities. Boats and cars are examples of liabilities because they fall in value the longer you own them and use them; they cost money to operate and maintain; and if you owe someone who lent you money to buy that boat or car, you could spend *even more* in interest expense than the original sticker price.

There are very, very few examples of "good debt" and even that can get you in financial trouble if you can't repay it when lenders expect to get paid, just like you can get evicted from your home if you fail to pay your landlord on time. Or have your car repossessed if you fail to make your car payments on time. Some agreements in finance allow lenders to take your company, sell your other stock investments and force you into bankruptcy if you fail to make even one payment. In other countries, you can be arrested and put in jail; that's something we did in the U.S. as recently as the 19th century. *Avoid* debt if you can, *prioritize* paying off any debt you must get and *manage* your budget and lifestyle so you can be a lender instead of a borrower. Stay on the good side of debt, don't pay royalties to the bankers for inventing debt, a tool that captures and enslaves productive society. Be wise and discipline yourself to save your earnings before you buy expensive things.

CHAPTER 6: THE CREDIT SCORE

<u>THE GPA FOR DEBT STUDIES</u>

If you ever get to a point where you need debt, you will be evaluated based on something called your *credit score*. A high credit score allows you to borrow the most amount of money at the lowest possible interest cost. A low credit score can prohibit you from accessing credit – getting a car loan, qualifying for a mortgage or even getting approved as a tenant by a new landlord. It's a lot like a GPA in high school, but since most people don't know much about it, they probably haven't done enough of the right things to make their score as high as possible. Please pay attention to this section and create habits that allow you to achieve the highest possible score *just in case* you might need to get credit or a loan for something along your life's financial journey.

If you are younger than 18 years old, you probably don't have a credit score yet – that's great! When you turn eighteen, credit card companies and stores where you shop will fall all over themselves to offer you a low credit limit card or account, something like $500 or maybe $2,500. That just means they are willing to take a small financial risk on you even though you are an *unproven credit risk* because you might just be responsible enough to pay them interest – remember, at 18% to 24% annually – for a very long time. What they don't know is that you are financially literate! You are going to accept their extension of credit and pay that booger off as soon as you get the bill because you already *budgeted* for the expense and *saved* enough to pay for it with cash!

The credit card companies, insurance companies and any merchant that extends you credit, including doctor's offices and dentists will report their *experience* with you to credit reporting agencies – Equifax, TransUnion and Experian – who track your unique identifying information like your social security number, birthdate, address, license number, etc. along with any reports of credit limits – how much credit you have been given; outstanding balances – how much credit you have actually used; and payment history – how consistently you have been paying down those balances. If you are late with a payment, you not only have to pay a late fee to the card company, but they also report that late payment to the agencies and your credit score drops like a rock.

The agencies use a few different methods for calculating your credit score, but the most common are the FICO – which stands for Fair Issac Corporation that developed the model – and VantageScore. They generally top out at 850 which is a meaningless number, but everything is relative. The closer your score is to 850, the more likely you are going to be given a *lot* of credit, or the *ability to borrow,* and probably will be offered the lowest interest rate available; you are an *excellent* credit. A score below 780 down to 660 will put you in a *good* category and this is where most Americans end up. The financially illiterate folks out there end up with scores down to 600 (*fair credit*), or down to 500 (*poor credit*) or even as low as 300 (*very poor credit risk*). If you have lower scores, you will have to pay exorbitant interest rates and that's *only if* you are approved for any small amount of credit. The credit models predict whether you are likely to repay your debts on time or whether you are likely to skip town and go bankrupt, leaving the store or credit card companies holding an empty bag of your promises to pay them back.

Other inputs to the credit score, in addition to your amount of credit available, amount used and payment history, include things like your income and asset levels. If you have high income, the agencies figure you can *afford* to take out more debt because you have more money each month to pay any amounts owed. If you borrow *all* the credit you have available to you – regardless of your income – that is an indication that you are not financially literate, and your score will drop because you may be spending *waaaay* more than you can ever pay back. Again, these credit score models are trying to predict if you are likely to *default* on a loan. There is a risk that you may not pay back the lender and they will have to spend more time and money to chase you down to collect. If things go really badly for them and you refuse to pay them back, they may have to sue you and obtain a legal judgment that allows them to *garnish* your wages or secure their eventual repayment from you by putting a *lien* on any real property or other assets you may own. Yes, they can do this because you signed the credit agreement in the store or when you accepted that credit card. Remember all the way back to the paycheck section: *garnishment* is one of those deductions that can occur from your gross income if you have judgments against you to collect money you owed but never paid. It also applies to things like unpaid rent or alimony and child support in cases where spouses get divorced and do not keep up the financial obligations agreed to in the divorce settlement. None of this is good for your credit score.

DEFAULTS AND BANKRUPTCY

The final straw for financially illiterate borrowers is something called *bankruptcy*. This is a legal process that allows individuals and companies to *discharge* many of the debts they have incurred because they can show a complete *inability* to repay those debts. Most lenders will try to work with borrowers to forgive penalties, reduce interest rates or lower monthly payment amounts in the hope that the borrower will at least make some progress toward repaying them. But at some point, the borrower quits trying and *files a petition* with a court to have their debts *expunged* or wiped out. Lenders hate this! The credit reporting agencies can see the court judgment in public records for seven to ten years, so they update their models and you become a *very poor credit risk*. If – and that's a very big IF – someone ever lends you money again, it will be a very small amount and very expensive. The lender may even require additional *security* like a lien on your property; in case you again fail to pay them back, they will just take your assets. Do not go down this route; it is a slippery slope from which it is increasingly harder to recover and rebuild trust in your creditworthiness. Bankruptcies are like dog poo on your shoes: you are tagged for almost a decade as a *deadbeat* borrower, and you lose that time to pursue your purpose. Money will be harder to earn because some of the best jobs – especially those in finance – look at your credit score as part of the hiring and vetting process. Why would an employer in finance believe you can do good work in that field if you can't pay your bills on time? Again, this is another reason you should avoid debt if you can and prioritize repaying that debt on time or even early so your credit score remains pristine.

CHAPTER 7: SAVING MONEY

A penny saved is a penny earned.

- Benjamin Franklin

Yeah, pretty soon you'll start thinking of this book as *Poor Richard's Quotable*! But you gotta give it to old Ben... he had all these cutesy quotes *and* got his mug on the front of a $100 dollar bill! My hero! What a guy! Or hey: maybe he got his face on the front of that bill *because* of his pithy one-liners. Hmm.

Right. So, when I was a kid, I was fascinated by all things medieval: knights, sword fighting and jousting, kings and crusades, but I especially liked castles; built one for show-and-tell in middle school. I would read and dream about the attacking offense with longbows, maces, pikes and catapults... so cool! Then I understood why the castles had all those great defenses: high walls, ramparts, boiling tar above the drawbridge... across a dragon-filled moat! Yeah, dragons!

FINANCIAL MOAT FOR DEFENSE

Where am I going with all this reverie? *Moats*, baby, that's where it's at! In personal finance, you can have a moat by building up savings. If you have savings, you can take a financial hit and still stay on track. Savings gives you some breathing room and reduces your stress and anxiety during financial turmoil. In the back of your mind and printed on your bank statement is an amount of money that you know is available to cover surprises like accidents, emergencies, and plain old bad luck... or even really nice things like a surprise weekend trip to Disney. Having a special pocket full of money provides a sense of security that you can handle those bumps in the road like a flat tire, torn suit jacket or car that won't start. Besides the relief of having an amount available for contingencies like these, getting that pile of money set aside has instilled in you another great habit of thriftiness: spending less than you earn so you have money available *when you need it*. The castle doesn't need thick, high walls and a broad mucky moat all the time – just when the invading hordes lay siege with dreams of sacking and pillaging and selling you something expensive you don't need.

THE DEBT HORDE

Philosophically, I'll continue to take the position that most debt is bad for most people most of the time. That leaves an awful lot of room for you to say you're the exception, and maybe that's true. Regardless, I encourage everyone to start out with no debt and stay that way for as long as possible. "But cars are expensive, so I have to borrow to buy one!" you say, and I'd respond, "No. You can save more for longer and pay all cash for a different car that is less expensive. You just have your mind, or more likely, your heart and self-image set on an expensive vehicle and you haven't been saving long enough to buy *that* particular car." *Where is the need* and at what point does it cross over into *want*? It is possible to buy cars without taking on a loan, it's just harder to find *that* deal. And *ugh!* you don't want dad's old hand-me-down clunker, what would your friends think? What would they think if you owned cars free-and-clear in each state where you own rental properties by the time you're 30 years old? If your priority is what your *friends* think, surround yourself with better friends or else plan on being poor and never achieving your purpose in life.

OK, I'll relax – a little – and agree that sometimes incurring debt is almost impossible to escape. So, you take out a loan or mortgage or debt to buy something you really need. Fine. Now what? Pay off that debt as quickly as you can because it is a claim on a (probably big) portion of your income and until the monthly payment obligation is satisfied, it will be a constant point of stress. It will also get worse if you *don't* make every monthly payment (late fees!) and if you lose your job or can't earn money for as long as the obligation to make those payments exists... you lose whatever you bought and probably some other assets you might have owned. You could even be forced into bankruptcy.

Bankruptcy, introduced in the earlier chapter, is a condition where you have more liabilities than assets and no clear path to paying off those liabilities because you cannot earn enough to pay them off. Our legal system has a process for *discharging* some debts, wiping them off so you are no longer responsible for them. That means the lender doesn't get paid what they are owed, so they tell everyone they know that you are a *bad credit* because they lost the money they lent to you to spend on something you couldn't afford. It's a low place to be in our society and makes life much harder for the next ten years in most cases. That's a huge set-back to achieving your life goals. The rest of this chapter will focus on how to avoid debt by saving that little bit that's left over when income remains greater than expenses, when you are living within your means and spending less than you earn. This is a comfortable place to thrive and will help you maintain a healthy lifestyle.

BUILD A SMALL MOAT

You've already built your budget and gave a lot of thought to which expenses are necessary and which ones you can do without. For example, let's pretend you have a job earning $1,000 each month, and you might have expenses that total on average $800 each month. Cool. Every month, you have an extra $200 left over since your income is greater than expenses. Well, you're at least financially literate at a fifth-grade level, congrats! (Don't be bummed out – that's better than most people in the U.S.!) You *can* spend that money on something new and shiny each month, but you *know* that's not where I'm headed. You *could* leave that balance in your bank account and in the next few months it'll be such a tantalizingly big amount that you buy something even bigger and shinier! But no, that would be a sixth or seventh grade mistake.

Let me encourage you to save at least $1,000 as soon as possible. Set it aside in a savings account or maybe even take it out as cash and put it somewhere safe that is out of sight. If you don't see it and tease yourself with how you can spend it, you might just keep it! There is no magic about having $1,000 but it is a reasonable goal that is achievable in a short(ish) period of time. The next hurdle is to keep it for a length of time and not dip into it for anything. Again, we are building habits with this exercise, so if you mess up and blow your budget one month and have to use some of your savings to cover your excessive spending, do it, review it, learn from it and build back better.

Paying off debt is tedious and takes far longer than you can imagine, but if you are diligent, you can do it and you will feel so much relief when it is done! One approach is to pay off the *highest interest rate* debt first. I favor this approach since each dollar of this outstanding debt costs you more than any other dollar of debt with a lower interest rate. Get rid of expensive liabilities first! However, another popular approach tackles the *smallest balance* debt first. This gives you a "quick win" and helps build your confidence to succeed in getting rid of each of your debts. Some folks like to *round up each payment* to the next $100 and still other folks will try to consolidate a whole bunch of small debts into one large debt. That might be OK if the new interest rate is lower than the weighted average of the existing debt, just be sure the new required monthly payment fits within your budget plan. Yes, there are a ton of books written on the topic of getting out of debt and most of them offer great ideas; find a method that works for you but remember how stressful all this debt is and simply avoid it all in the first place by building up your savings!

WIDEN THE MOAT

Keep that $1,000 for at least three full months and then pat yourself on the back. Now, if you have any existing debt, start paying that debt down with any extra savings that you can set aside each month. Part of your budget already includes the required monthly payment on existing debt, now you can add to that minimum payment and pay back more principal faster. Paying back principal lowers the amount of any interest that is accruing on that debt and enables you to pay down the principal even faster. Remember, you shouldn't have debt but if you do, prioritize paying it off.

DEEPEN THE MOAT

Congrats! You saved $1,000 without touching it for three whole months, not *too* hard, right? You are now well on your way to eliminating any remaining debt. OK, now save up *six months'* worth of your expenses. <GULP!> Yes, in our example, that is $800 times six which is $4,800. If you are saving $200 each month and you kept your $1,000 untouched for three months already, you have something like a $1,600 head start here, so only $3,200 more to go (divided by $200 each month)... Yes, it will take you almost one and a half years to save *only* six months' worth of your planned, or budgeted, expenses. Maybe reconsider how many of those expenses are *absolutely* necessary?

But why in the world do we need to *save* that much? Well, what happens if you lose your job? How quickly can you reduce your expenses back to zero each month? *That* is totally unreasonable and impractical. Alternatively, how long can you stretch that $1,000+ you now have in savings – *maybe* two months? If you got another, equally lucrative job super quickly, you might not miss a beat, but that doesn't happen very often. Or what if you got really sick or had a huge car accident that broke your neck or back and you couldn't work for a few months – *crunch*, there goes your savings and you might be stressing about meeting your budget again. On a really dark note, what if a family member died and you just didn't feel like you could make it to work and do a very good job at it? From a loss like that it can take a long time to regroup. Saving six months' worth of expenses is just good (un)common sense; it is wise to have enough set aside to survive until you can thrive again. We don't know what calamities may befall us in life, but if we save for the *potential* of bad things to happen, it won't really matter what *kind* of bad it is, we can stick within our budget and maybe lighten up on a few *wants* until we get our feet back under us and move forward again – in confidence and without taking on more debt. That's the power of the moat, of a solid defense against the invading debt hordes, of financial security in the face of desperate times. Bad things happen – to *everyone* and *more often* than we might expect – so plan to battle them on your own terms from a position of strength when those bad times do lay siege to your financial castle. Told you I love this medieval stuff!

PLAN AND SAVE FOR BIG TICKET ITEMS

Back to our example: it's been sixteen months, you're at least a year older, maybe you got a raise and increased your spending a little, but you have $4,800 in your savings account, wow! I'll bet saving $200 each month is so easy now it feels like, well, probably doesn't feel like much of anything if you're in the habit of doing it consistently for a year and a half. That's the goal right there! Saving must become so automatic that it doesn't even cross your mind, like looking both ways before crossing the street or reaching for your phone whenever you hear it ring.

The side benefit of saving for so long, for such a stretch goal as you just did, is that now you have a strong defense against unplanned emergencies. Given this recent experience, I would suggest you *earmark* the next few months' savings amounts for some kind of *planned expense*, something big but unavoidable. Think along the lines of a long vacation in an exotic locale, or a new(er) car. Maybe you're starting to think about getting married (ain't cheap, lemme tell ya!) or if you already own a home or condo, maybe you have some big repairs on the horizon or you just want to add a deck or update the kitchen. Whatever the "big expense" is, start *saving* to pay for it rather than *borrow debt* to buy it.

This is the secret to becoming wealthy: don't spend more due to interest costs for something you can buy with cash from your bank account because you've diligently been saving for a while. Occasionally, you will find that the big expense you were saving for so long to buy... isn't all that interesting now. Awesome! You broke the siren song of advertisers and marketers; you delayed your purchase long enough that it holds no sway over your emotions! That's a huge element of financial freedom and most people never get to experience that. Now, you are ahead of the class!

FILL THE MOAT WITH INKY WATER, POINTY STICKS, ALLIGATORS AND ORCS AFTER ENCHANTING IT WITH ACIDIC MUD THAT BURNS

Before you think that's it – all good with six months of expenses and an ability to save for big ticket items – there is just one last, small thing you should save for: *TWO YEARS' WORTH OF EXPENSES*. This is the end goal of your new habit. By the time you start working on this goal, of course, you will probably be earning more like $5,000 per month and your expenses will likely be more like $4,000 per month... lifestyle creep is a hard dragon to slay, so that moat needs to grow as well. As we get older, it takes longer to recover from unexpected emergencies like job loss or physical accidents and the unplanned expenses are usually much larger (why *wasn't* the foundation already *settled*? A new roof costs *how much!?*) than when we are younger with lower cost assets (aw, man, my ear buds don't work again). Also, by now you will have some experience investing in those retirement plan accounts so shift your emergency savings into very safe, very liquid assets like money market funds or short-term investment grade bond funds where you can earn a better interest rate than just a savings account. Make sure you can access these funds for their intended purpose – during an emergency – without waiting for days or paying withdrawal fees. You never know *when* you might need it, so make sure you can get it whenever the need eventually hits.

CHAPTER 8: INVESTING MONEY

Compound interest is the eighth wonder of the world. He who understands it, earns it; he who doesn't, pays it.

- Albert Einstein

Oh goody! Now we get to my favorite section – investing! When other kids clamored for the next new skateboard or drooled over some designer jeans and hella fresh kicks – yes, even when *I* was young, kids were obsessed with their drip – all I ever wanted was shares in MSFT. Wait, that's not even a word, I have to remind myself sometimes to stop talking in code. MSFT is the *ticker symbol* for Microsoft Corporation. Remember when I said I learned how to code as a young tweenager at a junior college? I was learning BASIC, and I thought it was so cool and so easy that the company that made it was going to be *absolutely huge*! Well, it had just gone public earlier that year, 1986 for those of you keeping track, and it was already big, but then they got smaller, and then they got bigger, and then too big so the Justice Department made them smaller again, and now... Today, as I write the intro to this chapter, Microsoft is the *largest* company in the world with a market capitalization of almost $3.1 *trillion*. If I could have bought, or gotten my parents to buy, *$100 worth* of MSFT instead of those Girbaud jeans (which I still have and wear, so at least the average cost there is pretty minimal), I would have almost $500,000 worth of MSFT. Rats! Curse that lifestyle gene *and jeans*!

ACQUIRE ASSETS, COMPOUND RETURNS
Investing is the, uh... er, scientific art? of buying ASSETS that go up in value over time and generate CASH FLOW, which is a fancy way of

saying positive cash returns. LIABILITIES, on the other hand, are things that usually lose value or cost more money to maintain once you own them, which should sound a lot like *debt* by now. A lease or rent is also considered a liability because you are obligated to make continual payments according to a contract, therefore, it is a *use* or *drain* on the cash that would otherwise still be an asset in your bank account. We will cover assets and liabilities in more detail when we discuss NET WORTH or NET WEALTH and dive more deeply into FINANCIAL STATEMENTS which summarize these kinds of things, both for individuals and for companies, even governments in a weird way. For now, remember we *invest* our cash, or capital, in *assets* because we expect their value to increase over time.

GAMBLING AND SPECULATION

Speculation and gambling[*] do not qualify as investments. Gambling is placing a bet with some statistical probability for either winning more than is *wagered* or else losing the entire amount of the wager. Most *legal gambling* does have a statistical payout; alas, that expected payout, or return, is *always* less than the wager... and that's before the house takes its *vigorish*. Speculation is putting money into something for which there is *no way* to make a reasonable *forecast* for the return of your money. That is a critically important distinction: assets have current value and generate additional cash returns over time and may also increase in value over time; whereas with a speculative investment, we cannot be sure what the value is today, it might not generate any additional cash returns over time and there is no way to forecast *when or even if* we might be able to get our capital returned. Some examples of gambling and speculation include lottery tickets (since the expected return is often pennies per dollar paid for the ticket), trading cards (who still has their collection of Pokeman, be honest!), and even cryptocurrencies are considered highly speculative. For each of these examples, how much is it likely to be worth in one year? Based on what assumptions? What legal standing do they have to serve as an exchange of value? One last warning on speculation is a... what to call it, movement? an organization? that calls itself multi-level marketing. Less prevalent today but still out there in many forms, these are basically Ponzi schemes. You give me money today and I give you a product that you can sell for many times your "investment" by getting other people to buy it from you to sell to other people at many times *their* "investment"... rinse and repeat. It has been done with makeup, dietary supplements, international calling cards (yeah, that's one for the history books), water filters and even Tupperware! These are not investments, they are scams. And yes, sometimes some people make money on these. You don't need to go down this route now that you are financially literate; there are plenty of other careers.

COMPOUND INTEREST

OK, boss, no gambling, speculating or Ponzi schemes; but why do people invest and how does it work? The simplest way to demonstrate the concept is to understand *compound interest*. If you want to save $1,000 – great idea! – and have only $200 to start, you can find a savings account that will pay you an annual interest rate of 1% *compounded monthly*. After the first month you maintain the balance, the bank will add $0.17 (rounded) to your account. That's not much, how did they decide it was $0.17? It is the same idea that bankers use to figure out how much interest you owe them on your debt: 1% annualized interest divided by twelve (months in a year) times the $200 balance is $0.17. OK, what about next month? You add $200 to the $200.17 in your account and the bank pays you $0.33 in interest for a total of $400.50 at the end of the second month. Your goal is $1,000 in savings, so you add $200 every month in addition to the interest that the bank pays you to leave your money in the account. Now, after five months you've saved $1,000 and your ending account total is $1,002.50, and every month after that the bank pays you at least $1 to leave your money in the account.

As you play with the compound interest spreadsheet, you should begin to see a very powerful pattern. The higher the starting dollar amount or the higher the interest rate or the more constant the additional contributions to the interest-bearing balance... the more interest or *return* will accrue to your net wealth. Instead of only 1%, change the interest you earn to 5% and look out in time to five years, which is 60 months. Remember the earlier car loan example, where you borrowed $22,500 at 12% interest and made $500 monthly payments for five years? Look at it from the angle of *saving* $500 monthly at 5% interest:

Compound Interest - Always Working (for or against you!)

		Added Money	Cumulative	Interest Earned	5% annually End Balance
1	Jun-24	$ 200.00	$ 200.00	$ 0.83	$ 200.83
2	Jul-24	$ 200.00	$ 400.83	$ 1.67	$ 402.50
3	Aug-24	$ 200.00	$ 602.50	$ 2.51	$ 605.01
4	Sep-24	$ 200.00	$ 805.01	$ 3.35	$ 808.37
5	Oct-24	$ 200.00	$ 1,008.37	$ 4.20	$ 1,012.57
6	Nov-24	$ 200.00	$ 1,212.57	$ 5.05	$ 1,217.62

Instead of spending more than $30,000 in payments for a loan, you could have saved an extra $4,100 as the interest you earned compounded to earn even more interest every month. Alternatively, you would have to contribute only $440 each month compounding at 5% to achieve the same $30,041 you spent on the Chrysler 300 loan. Neat, eh?

		Added Money	Cumulative	Interest Earned	5% annually End Balance
1	Jun-24	$ 500.00	$ 500.00	$ 2.08	$ 502.08
2	Jul-24	$ 500.00	$ 1,002.08	$ 4.18	$ 1,006.26
3	Aug-24	$ 500.00	$ 1,506.26	$ 6.28	$ 1,512.53
4	Sep-24	$ 500.00	$ 2,012.53	$ 8.39	$ 2,020.92
5	Oct-24	$ 500.00	$ 2,520.92	$ 10.50	$ 2,531.42
6	Nov-24	$ 500.00	$ 3,031.42	$ 12.63	$ 3,044.06
...	...	...	...	...	...
59	Apr-29	$ 500.00	$ 33,364.02	$ 139.02	$ 33,503.04
60	May-29	$ 500.00	$ 34,003.04	$ 141.68	$ 34,144.72

Lastly, for one mind-blowing moment, now look ahead 20 years, and then 50 years. Go back to saving just $200 every month for 50 years and earning only 5% annually: it adds up to $533,730! Now, you're pretty quick with math and just figured out $200/month times 600 months (50 years) is only $120,000... so how is the balance in your account over *half a million dollars*!? Well, in addition to paying you interest on your capital deposits, they pay interest on *all the prior periods' interest payments*! This starts an *exponential* earnings bonanza! Welcome to the gooey, lovely, awesome power of *compound interest*. Are you as smitten as I am? (Sigh...)

But why would a bank ever pay out more than $415,000 in interest when you only put in $120,000? Indeed*. Banks are just a business, and they are in the business of *borrowing* cheap money from your savings account and *lending* that money out dearly. That's a fancy way of saying "at a much higher interest rate" than they pay you. The bank earns a "net interest margin" between your 1% or 5% interest rate and their clients' borrowing rate for things like boats and cars and credit cards and mortgages and other business loans, usually a *spread* of more than 3% to 8% over the amount they pay you. But wait! Sometimes aren't *you* on the other side of that relationship, too? Absolutely! This is why I say avoid debt, use your own money to buy things, even expensive things! You'll *earn* the return by saving instead of *paying* the return by borrowing.

Interest **expense** is a **cost** of borrowing.

Interest **income** is a **return** on savings and investments.

Perhaps now Einstein's quote makes a little more sense? Perhaps there's a little motivation and excitement around saving today, earning a return and then having *even more* money later to buy the big things you might want to buy? This is incredible knowledge, powerful knowledge. Like understanding physics, chemistry, *and* math but also knowing how to sing, write well, and speak to large audiences.

ASSET CLASSES AND PORTFOLIOS

Take a break and bask in the glory that is compound interest. Think about all the ways it can love you for the rest of your life and give you everything you ever wanted... OK, now come back to reality and understand that investing is earning a return on as many assets as you can collect. The more you can compound those returns, the faster you will build wealth. There are many categories of assets, called asset classes, which generate different levels of return for compounding: bonds and equities, for example. You may consider your house as part of your portfolio. Professional investors strive to *balance* their holdings across as many different assets as possible because it minimizes something they don't like called RISK. Not the game. But that's fun, too.

In real LIFE (another fun game!), the idea of investing lives hand-in-hand with *risk*. Risk can be defined across dozens of parameters, but the one most finance folks are worried about is volatility: how much the value of an investment goes up or down in a given period of time, like one year. The really cool thing about asset classes is they each have different volatility (risk) profiles and combining them into a single portfolio reduces the overall or combined volatility experience. In other words, you can earn a more consistent return without suffering the gut-wrenching swings in asset prices.

BANKS AND BONDS♪: FIXED INCOME

Cash has extremely low volatility: a dollar is basically worth a dollar all year long. Inflation reduces what it can buy over time, so even cash isn't zero volatility, but it's the closest thing to zero volatility that exists. One way to think of it: the rate you earn on a bank savings account almost compensates for the decline in value due to inflation. Slightly more volatile are things called long U.S. government bonds with a maturity, say, of more than five years away and often up to thirty years. Company bonds of the same time to maturity are even more risky because there isn't a government guarantee backed by the ability to print more dollars, just a promise from a profit-seeking company that you will get your interest and principal back. Principal, remember, is just the *borrowed amount* of capital. So, now you know principal, interest, and term to maturity, which is sometimes referred to as duration but that's actually a far more technical term more like a weighted average... never mind, stay on target; these are the primary elements of fixed income investing.

Bank savings accounts are the simplest form of compound interest, the easiest way to wrap your head around the concept so you can apply it to other investments. Bonds, also called *fixed income* are very similar: instead of putting *capital* in the bank, you *buy* a piece of paper called a bond *issued* by a government or trustworthy company that pays you interest for a period of time before you are repaid the original bond amount. It is the same thing as *lending* the money to a bank, a government or company because they promise to pay you back the *principal,* the <u>return of</u> the original amount of capital you lent them upfront by buying their bond, in addition to the ongoing interest cost (to them) which is your <u>return on</u> capital. See? You are now a lender earning a return on your capital! To make the return *truly compound* you would have to *reinvest* each interest payment into another bond. You would be very busy indeed if you had to do it this way, but the idea is to *invest capital*, say $1,000 every month into new bonds that pay interest, typically twice a year rather than every month, and constantly *reinvest* larger and larger amounts each period because you are constantly getting interest and some of your capital back every period as different bonds mature and pay back the original capital you lent them.

The term fixed income refers to the fixed amount of interest payments owed by the borrower to a lender, determined once the bond is offered, or *issued*, to the market. The issue is thereafter referred to as "the 7.5% 2055 US Government bond" or "3.25% 2030 JP Morgan debenture" or what have you. That interest rate is *fixed* for the term over which the bond is outstanding. Weirdly, even floating rate notes and loans are included in the fixed income asset class. Oh well, nobody ever promised to make investing easy to understand!

If some of the terms or concepts on fixed income investing are confusing here, do not stress. There is more detail and a fair amount of repetition in Chapter 11 to help cement these ideas better and with a broader perspective. For now, just grasp the main ideas and distinctions between debt and equity.

STOCKS ARE EQUITIES

Stocks are interchangeably referred to as equities and equity is just a fancy term for ownership which is a different asset class than fixed income. Whereas loans and bonds are *debt obligations* of companies and governments and individuals, *equity* represents a shared claim on *all future residual cash flows* of a business. If a company sold everything it made, covered its costs of operating, paid all its taxes, paid off its debts and still had money left over – profits – then each owner would get a proportional share of whatever is left over. If you owned 100 shares of a company that had one billion shares of ownership, you would own 0.000001% of that company. If they liquidated and had $1 billion left over, you'd get $100. Meh. So, most investors want to buy companies – that really, really small share they can afford – which are *going concerns* meaning they are expected to stay in business and generate ongoing profits. Profits can either be *distributed* to shareholders by way of *dividends* or *stock repurchases*, or else they can be *reinvested* into new machines to lower costs, introduce new products or buy other fast-growing businesses. In this way, equities can be thought of as an infinitely long bond that pays out a hopefully growing pile of profits (rather than a fixed interest rate) to shareholders. If the company keeps those profits, the expectation is that the stock price will increase at a *compounding rate* as the company generates even *more* profits on those profits – this concept *better* sound familiar by now! The result of all those compounding profits is an increase in the value of the stock price.

Notice how this differs from speculation: we have an expectation and an ability to forecast ongoing returns *and* an eventual liquidation price of the company we own, thus we refer to this as equity investing. If the companies we own never liquidate but we need cash to buy something, we can always sell some or all of the equities we own back to other buyers. This buying and selling occurs in the *public stock market*. While we won't go into too much detail on that here, it is worth learning more about its fascinating history and state of current affairs.

Most people are at least aware of stocks and bonds, but too many of those folks think it is out of reach for them to invest, or they are afraid that it is too confusing for them, too risky. The reality is that most people *should* invest in the public markets for equities and fixed income because it is the best way to get their capital working for *them* instead of them working for *it*! When you work a job and get paid, you are just earning money. The distinction is slight but here's how you should think about it: capital is investment money; money is just spending money. When someone asks, "how much money do you have?" you can now say, "only what's in my budget" or "not much!" But when someone financially literate asks, "how much capital do you have to invest?" you can answer "*Gobs!*" Or actually, don't. Cuz then they'll just want to "manage it for you" and charge you a lot of fees to advise you how to invest it. This book will discuss various ways to invest in the markets on your own; it's simple, fun and quite inexpensive to do yourself.

REAL ESTATE

Let's talk first, though, about another asset class called *real estate*, probably one of my favorites! A home is real estate you live in, like a house or condo and apartment buildings. A car, boat or mobile home is *not* considered real estate; rather, it is personal property. *So many* books have been written about real estate investing, it feels a bit awkward working it in to this book, but it is so fundamentally important to increasing your net wealth, I just couldn't ignore it. People who pay rent their entire lives are *spending* money on shelter; people who buy a home – condo, single family house, duplex, etc. – to live in are *investing* in their own shelter. It isn't bad to rent, especially if you can split the cost of the place with roommates, but it's almost always better to own your home.

Rent is a much lower *upfront cost*, since buying a home requires what is called a *down payment* plus a mortgage, or else enough saved cash to buy the place outright. In the earlier car loan example, you paid a $2,500 *down payment* to drive it off the lot. The rest of the purchase price was borrowed. A *home mortgage* is the same concept: it is the debt you incur to pay the seller the rest of the purchase price after your down payment. Most mortgages require 20% down, though some will allow 10%, 5% or even as little as 2% but those come with higher costs for insurance in addition to a higher interest rate. Rent is easy: fixed amount every month for a specified period of time, like a year, or month-by-month. If you buy your home, you have to pay property taxes and maintenance, but any smart landlord has already priced those things into the rent you're paying, so in reality you are already paying for those things, you just don't have to feel responsible for them. Toilet clogged? Call the super'. With your own home, you are on the hook for repairs, but you get to benefit from increases in the home's value over time.

You should read a few introductory books on real estate, think about the choice between renting and buying, and expose yourself to the idea of eventually investing in rental properties because this is a route that individuals can use to easily increase their net wealth over many, many years. Create a compound interest table like we did in the previous chapter: use today's value of your rented place as estimated on Zillow or Redfin as the starting contribution; if you're in an apartment, find a nearby condo that might be comparable and use that value instead. Depending on the city you live in, real estate values have typically increased by 3% - 8% annually over the past 30 years, with maybe a few years of smaller, negative returns. See how much the place would be worth in five years or ten years or thirty years at a constant 3% or 8% annual appreciation.

Real Estate Appreciation Estimate

		Added Money	Cumulative	Appreciation 3% annually	End Balance
1	Jun-24	$ 400,000	$ 400,000	$ 1,000	$ 401,000
2	Jul-24	$ -	$ 401,000	$ 1,003	$ 402,003
3	Aug-24	$ -	$ 402,003	$ 1,005	$ 403,008
4	Sep-24	$ -	$ 403,008	$ 1,008	$ 404,015
5	Oct-24	$ -	$ 404,015	$ 1,010	$ 405,025
6	Nov-24	$ -	$ 405,025	$ 1,013	$ 406,038
...	...	...	...	...	...
59	Apr-29	$ -	$ 462,332	$ 1,156	$ 463,488
60	May-29	$ -	$ 463,488	$ 1,159	$ 464,647
...	...	...	...	...	...
119	Apr-34	$ -	$ 537,053	$ 1,343	$ 538,395
120	May-34	$ -	$ 538,395	$ 1,346	$ 539,741
...	...	...	...	...	...
359	Apr-54	$ -	$ 977,842	$ 2,445	$ 980,286
360	May-54	$ -	$ 980,286	$ 2,451	$ 982,737

Wow! That $400,000 home is worth more than $1 million by December of 2054 assuming only 3% annualized appreciation and ten times the original value at 8%!

		Added Money	Cumulative	Appreciation	8% annually End Balance
1	Jun-24	$ 400,000	$ 400,000	$ 2,667	$ 402,667
2	Jul-24	$ -	$ 402,667	$ 2,684	$ 405,351
3	Aug-24	$ -	$ 405,351	$ 2,702	$ 408,053
4	Sep-24	$ -	$ 408,053	$ 2,720	$ 410,774
5	Oct-24	$ -	$ 410,774	$ 2,738	$ 413,512
6	Nov-24	$ -	$ 413,512	$ 2,757	$ 416,269
...	...	...	...	...	...
59	Apr-29	$ -	$ 588,071	$ 3,920	$ 591,992
60	May-29	$ -	$ 591,992	$ 3,947	$ 595,938
...	...	...	...	...	...
119	Apr-34	$ -	$ 876,135	$ 5,841	$ 881,976
120	May-34	$ -	$ 881,976	$ 5,880	$ 887,856
...	...	...	...	...	...
359	Apr-54	$ -	$ 4,316,546	$ 28,777	$ 4,345,323
360	May-54	$ -	$ 4,345,323	$ 28,969	$ 4,374,292

Now plug in your rent as the ongoing monthly contribution, maybe haircut it by 20% for all the property taxes and maintenance expenses but increase the base rent rate by 5% every year which is typical. Say you currently pay $2,400/month in rent, about 7% annually of the home's value is the right ballpark. Check the value at year 30 again.

		Added Money	Cumulative	Appreciation	3% annually End Balance
1	Jun-24	$ 400,000	$ 400,000	$ 1,000	$ 401,000
2	Jul-24	$ 2,000	$ 403,000	$ 1,008	$ 404,008
3	Aug-24	$ 2,000	$ 406,008	$ 1,015	$ 407,023
4	Sep-24	$ 2,000	$ 409,023	$ 1,023	$ 410,045
5	Oct-24	$ 2,000	$ 412,045	$ 1,030	$ 413,075
6	Nov-24	$ 2,000	$ 415,075	$ 1,038	$ 416,113
...	...	...	...	...	...
59	Apr-29	$ 2,431	$ 599,247	$ 1,498	$ 600,745
60	May-29	$ 2,431	$ 603,176	$ 1,508	$ 604,684
...	...	...	...	...	...
119	Apr-34	$ 3,103	$ 876,465	$ 2,191	$ 878,656
120	May-34	$ 3,103	$ 881,758	$ 2,204	$ 883,963
...	...	...	...	...	...
359	Apr-54	$ 8,232	$ 3,267,243	$ 8,168	$ 3,275,411
360	May-54	$ 8,232	$ 3,283,644	$ 8,209	$ 3,291,853

Double wow! This would suggest a net wealth of $3.3 million from owning a $400,000 home and charging someone $2,400 in rent, paying 20% of that in expenses and plowing that money back into more real estate that appreciates at 3%. Crazy, but totally realistic. Many investors will put mortgages on each rental property which allows them to buy more property, but at the expense of interest every month. This approach requires less up-front (instead of $400,000, they put $80,000 to $160,000 down and borrow the rest) but increases the risk of defaulting on the debt, losing the house and initial down payment if you can't find tenants willing to pay enough to cover the mortgage and other carrying expenses of the property.

Personally, I started buying dirt-cheap, run-down homes as rental properties while I was still in college; I still own the first one I bought! I also still own the first condo I bought after business school. Living by myself was cool, but I rented out the second-floor loft to my college buddy who continued to live there for *eight years* after I moved out, all the while paying rent that covered almost my entire mortgage. When he bought his own place, I rented to a family that lived there *another 15 years* (so far... they still live there)! This is why your landlord loves you and wants you to keep renting forever: he is getting wealthy off your inability or unwillingness to save enough to buy your own place and *invest* in your own shelter.

Homes are a unique investment because you get personal *utility* – you live there! – from a financial asset, real estate. In fact, despite the risk of the home's value possibly going down for one or a few years, you aren't forced to sell it *as long as* you can afford the mortgage payments every month, *and* you *still* get to live in it whether it is worth more or less than you originally paid. That utility, or the ability to use something, has value in and of itself. And yes, home prices do go up *and down*, so watch the housing market where you live, or where you *think* you might want to live someday, and over many years, you will be able to spot a great deal when someone sells a place too cheap, at the bottom of a *market cycle*. If you are saving for a potential big purchase, you might just have enough money to snap it up and turn it into a rental or move into it and turn your current place into a rental! Again, there are a ton of books on this practice, and I would encourage you to spend some time reading them and thinking through whether this is one way of investing which appeals to you. It works for so many "millionaires next door" that I suspect many of you will try it.

COMMODITIES

Commodities are things that are consumed in the manufacture and production of other things, or in some cases they are just consumed directly – like coffee beans! There are dozens of commodities traded using a *contract* called a *futures*, or *forwards* in the case of interest rates and foreign currencies. While there are several *very* technical books on the different kinds of *physical* or *financial* futures, how to value them and how to structure various trades to make money using them, most businesses use them to ensure a specific cost for their raw materials or produced goods. Oil and natural gas are the most commonly traded *energy* commodities, as you might expect since they are inputs to virtually everything we make and do, and they get produced into gasoline and diesel which are also traded in futures markets. Copper and silver are popular *metals* that are traded as are steel, iron, aluminum and other precious metals. Then there is the *agricultural complex* including corn, soybeans, sugar, cotton, wheat, cocoa... and coffee! Yum!

CASH AND FX

The largest markets of all are Cash and FX, which stands for foreign currency exchange. These markets are not typically for individual investors, but they are absolutely, mind-bogglingly *huge* and constantly in motion; literally, there is never a minute when these are not being traded somewhere in the world. Cash markets are where banks and governments manage their cash needs or their excess cash. The Fed here in the U.S. represents a group of large *money center banks* who coordinate something called the *overnight rate for repo lending* (which stands for *repurchase obligation*) and otherwise set the target for interest rates at which the government will borrow or lend. These are technical aspects of the economy, stuff that goes on under the hood and that most people will never need to understand, but it is worth reading about because what goes on in these markets can have tremendous impacts on all financial markets – especially those like the stock and bond markets.

Foreign currencies are *priced* in microseconds all day, every day because we live in a global economy and businesses always need to buy something from another country or exchange the currency from another country in which they sold a product into their *local* or *home currency*. For instance, when you buy an Audi here in the U.S. and pay dollars, Volkswagon, based in Germany, is going to want euros to pay all their employees and shareholders. At any point in time, they can look up how many dollars it takes to buy a euro, and someone will exchange those two currencies for them. Individually, you do this at a very small level whenever you travel to another country and exchange some money for local spending money. You will notice two prices are always quoted: one price at which the exchange will *buy* your dollars, and another price at which they will *sell* you dollars. The difference is called a *spread* and it is the way they make a profit providing that service, usually in addition to a service fee. Conceptually, it is no different than buying a box of 20 candy bars for $10 and selling them to your neighbors at $1 each. The spread between your cost ($0.50) and the sales price ($1) is your profit. FX (Foreign eXchange) is just buying and selling other currencies, hopefully for a profit. Pretty neat, but unless you are a hawala, this probably is not a priority investment market to learn about until you become a pro. Then you'll know what a hawala is, too.

DIRECT EQUITIES INVESTING

Switch gears now and return to the equities asset class. There are many different methods for investing in equities. I'll get into more detail on *how* to buy and sell these things in a bit, but for now just know it is easy to do. The most obvious way is to buy a single company's *direct issue* shares, like I mentioned with MSFT. A lot of people who invest really enjoy *owning* a company they know and love, like SBUX or AMZN or TSLA and they can build up a *portfolio* of dozens of individual names. This is great... to a point. Another important concept to know when investing is *diversification* which just means not putting all your eggs in one basket. If you *only* invested in one stock like GME (that's Gamestop, if you didn't already know), the value of your investment portfolio would swing wildly up and down based just on the price of that one stock. Not a fun ride. Empirical evidence, that just means well-studied by academics, suggests that a well-diversified portfolio is one that has about 30 different names, beyond that you're just buying *beta*. OK, that was another technical term that I just couldn't avoid using, but it basically means you're pretty much buying the average of the market volatility. Not a bad thing, but there is an easier way to accomplish that called *index funds*.

INDEX INVESTING

Usually, when folks mention what happened in "the market" they are referring to an index, like S&P 500, NASDAQ 100 or Dow Jones Industrial Average; however, there are literally hundreds of different indexes, all created by various companies who claim to be selling a better mousetrap. Not literally mousetraps, of course, but the metaphor is subtly apropos. An index is simply a curated collection of individual equity positions held in various *weights* relative to the other equities in that index. In theory, for example, the S&P 500 is a *market capitalization weighted* list of the biggest 500 companies listed on any of the U.S. stock exchanges.

Yes, there is more than one exchange (NYSE, NASDAQ, PHLX, NSX, etc.) and when combined, they comprise the ambiguously named stock market... in air quotes. You don't have to concern yourself with which exchange lists which company because "technology" just whisks your buy-sell order to the appropriate place where someone wants to trade with you. So cool.

To buy an entire index means your investment will go up or down nearly as much as that index does. If 420 of those holdings, or individual stocks, go up and the other 80 names go down, the weighted average of all those holdings times each of their price changes, is your investment's daily price change, or performance. And yes, it is more technical than that since each index is often changing or being *rebalanced* or *reconstituted*, but the big idea is to give one-stop diversification. Most retirement plans offer multiple passive index options so you can easily choose to invest in the equities pie by way of large cap slices, small cap slices, value slices or some other common characteristic. Any brokerage will also provide a way to screen offerings across a dizzying array of indexes.

PASSIVE APPROACH VERSUS ACTIVE APPROACH

Holding an index position or multiple different indexes is considered *passive* indexing, even though you may *actively* trade in and out of different indexes, your portfolio consists of a defined exposure to various companies. Index investing is awesome because it is so cheap, and they tend to outperform almost all other forms of investing over long periods of time! On the other end of the *passive* spectrum is *active* investing.

MUTUAL FUNDS AND EXCHANGE TRADED FUNDS

Most *mutual funds* promote themselves as active investors who are better at picking which stocks to hold in the portfolio to *outperform the market* or some more relevant index called a *benchmark*. Fund shops and the people who manage each fund believe they have a *strategy*, a *secret sauce,* an *edge* or better information to forecast which stocks are going to go up the most and they will actively try to avoid those stocks they expect will go down. These funds charge much higher fees for advertising their prowess and doing all this work, of course, and if you buy some shares in their fund, they will just take their fees right out of your returns – or out of your capital if they end up being wrong and post a negative return. Alas, most retirement plans are full of *active mutual fund* options for investing in equities and bonds. You should compare the fees they each charge to the passive option, if you get one, for each category. That amount of fee difference, over many years, and with as much money as you are going to stuff into them after applying the principles of this book... will add up to *thousands of dollars* that you won't have in retirement! Now maybe those active funds can post better returns some quarters and some years, but over the very long period of time you will be investing, there are very, *very* few active mutual funds that have *ever* performed better than some of the most basic passive index funds over ten years or more. The typical difference in performance is usually much worse than the difference in fees.

Another thing about mutual funds is that they are *priced* at the end of the day when most stock markets have closed. After the market closes, the fund tallies up all their equity positions (2,000 shares of MSFT, 45 shares of META, etc.), multiplies by the ending price of those stocks and divides by the number of *outstanding* mutual fund shares that investors can own. The resulting amount is the price that mutual fund can be either bought or sold.

By the way, that's why it's called a mutual fund, everybody in that fund *mutually* owns all the underlying holdings. Imagine a mutual fund that sold $1 billion of shares to a million investors, then went out and bought $1 billion worth of diversified equities. Assume each original mutual fund share was worth $10. At the end of the next day, say the holdings are worth $1.1 billion – a 10% return in one day! Do some math and each mutual fund share is now worth... yes! $11, well, minus the fund management fee of 1% on an annual basis, so really only $10.99. Whenever you want to sell (or buy), you put in your order but you won't know what the price will be until the end of the day. *Exchange Traded Funds* (ETFs) are only different in the sense that you can trade those suckers as quickly as you hit submit during market hours. ETFs can hold the same weights of stocks, and they can be either passive indexes or actively traded strategies, and weirdly, they tend to be slightly cheaper than most mutual funds. ETFs are frequently coming out with more specificity in the kinds of exposures they offer; do your research, evaluate the cost and liquidity and try not to get too cute with your portfolio. It is really hard to beat the broad market passive index.

LONG POSITION VERSUS SHORT POSITION

I'll probably get in trouble for this next bit, but I think it's interesting and worth knowing, even if you never get into it. Almost everyone who buys stocks owns them *long*. That means if the stocks go up their portfolio increases in value, and vice versa. Pretty straightforward. Some investors – and yes, this is still investing – will *borrow* the stock through a stockbroker and immediately *sell* that same stock to some other investor. Later, they have to *buy* that same amount of stock back from the market and return it to the stockbroker from whom they originally *borrowed* it.

Why in the world would they do that? Well, if they borrowed a stock and sold it away, they are *short* that stock, meaning they have to eventually go back out, get it and return it. If that stock price goes *down* before they have to return it, they can buy it in the market *at a lower price than they originally sold it* and they get to keep the difference once they return the borrowed stock to the stockbroker or original owner. *Shorting the market* is a way to express an expectation that the price of the market, or asset, or company, or debt, or index, whatever will be lower at some point in the near future and that they will be able to buy it back cheaper.

The big risk for a short investor is if the stock continues to *increase* in value while they hold their short position; in that case, they may have to buy back the stock at a much higher price than they originally sold it to the market, often called a *short squeeze*. Ouch! Oh, and by the way, you have to pay what's called a *borrow fee* which is basically an annualized interest rate for *each day* you are short, and popular shorts are super expensive – like 10% or even 20%. Bummer! There are more than a few books written on this topic called *long-short* investing and it is a strategy executed by professionals who operate special investment vehicles called *hedge funds* which we will touch on again much later.

OPTIONS AND FUTURES INVESTING

Yet another way to acquire assets, predominantly in the equity market, is by using *options*. These – and futures which we referenced during the commodities discussion – are referred to broadly as *derivatives* because they *derive* their value and characteristics from the *underlying* asset. A *call option* is an *opportunity to buy* a given stock at a given price during a specific time. Without getting too technical, you can *exercise* your option if the price of the underlying asset rises above your *strike price* when you own a *call* option. The *counterparty* who *sold* you that call option is then obligated to *sell* you the underlying at the *strike price* even though the stock now sells for a higher price in the market.

Another kind of option is named a *put* option. If you *bought* a put option on a stock that *declines* in price *below* your strike price, you can *exercise* your option and *put* the underlying stock to a counterparty at the strike price even though the price of the stock is lower. Why in the world, again, would people do this?! Options are a way of expressing a view on the *direction* and *magnitude* of a stock price's expected movement. There are many ways to buy *and* sell fancy combinations of options to generate returns on the movement of a stock's price.

Again, most people buy and hold a stock long, but options are a way for professional investors to express a view and earn a return without holding the actual stock long or going through the complexity of borrowing and selling short. They create a *derivative* position using options. The options themselves have value, so they cost something called the *option price* or *premium*, but you can either buy it or sell it. If you sell a call option on stock you already own, you are paid the option premium upfront and if the price of the underlying stock doesn't exceed the strike price, then you get to keep the premium and your stock. If you sell a call option for stock you already own and the strike price is exceeded, the option *buyer,* your counterparty, will exercise their option and you will be forced to sell your stock at the strike price even though the market price is higher. You still get to keep the premium.

Alternatively, if you sell a put option, you again receive a premium and if the stock does not decline below the strike price, you keep the premium and you don't have to *buy* the underlying stock. But if you sold that put option and the price declines below the strike price, the counterparty will exercise their option and you will be forced to *buy* the underlying stock at the strike price. Similarly, if you *buy* a put option for stock you already own, you have to *pay* the premium and if the stock doesn't drop below the strike price, that's it. You don't exercise your option and you keep the stock you own. If you buy a put option and the price declines below the strike price, you exercise your option and force the counterparty to pay you more than the stock is priced in the market. Et cetera through all the permutations.

Professional investors can use these derivatives to *manage risk* in the portfolio which means they can reduce the impact of unexpected outcomes by paying premiums for options to buy or sell securities at known prices regardless what the market does. They can also generate premium income by selling options and managing that portfolio depending on what the price of the underlying securities does. By the way, you don't have to hold options until they expire, you can *close out* an option position before expiry by doing the reverse transaction (sell if you bought or buy if you sold) at whatever price is then in effect for that specific option. Lots of books have been written on derivatives and especially with respect to options; if this interests you, read them before getting over your skis with real money.

Futures were alluded to earlier during the discussion of commodities. The main idea is locking in a *future* price at which you will buy or sell the underlying, typically a commodity, but maybe an interest rate or currency. It is a contract to transact a very specific amount of a very specific thing at a specific location and at a defined time in the future. A bacon producer wants a million pounds of lean hogs of a specific quality, delivered in Chicago on December 15th so they can produce 500,000 two-pound packages of bacon-wrapped whatsits in time for Super Bowl parties. But it's July and they want to lock in the price now. Keeping it simple, futures market participants only put up a very small percentage of the agreed upon transaction price today and then if the price of the underlying commodity drifts down until *delivery* the party with a negative impact must *post* a small difference called *margin* on a daily basis to make up the change in price. This kind of investing is dangerous because there is significant *leverage* allowed, meaning you put up very little capital like $1,000 but control a massive position like $50,000. Just know the futures market exists and helps the economy run smoothly. Again though, if this topic fascinates you, study it thoroughly before risking much hard-earned capital trading it.

So far in this chapter, we've covered a lot of different ideas: compound interest; the differences between gambling', speculating and investing; and the difference between assets and liabilities are the three overarching concepts understood by people who are financially literate. Then we dove right in and discussed various asset classes which make up typical investments. We talked about some of the *products* that make it easy to own or participate in some of those assets as their prices move. Here is a good place to describe how exactly to go about buying these things since they don't usually go on sale at the grocery store, the mall, late night tele, WMT, TGT or COST (well, now Costco sells physical ounces of gold, so there's that).

<u>INVESTMENT ACCOUNTS ARE VEHICLES FOR INVESTING</u>

The easiest way to start investing is through your employer's retirement plan: a 401k or 403b for most folks. Remember, you are setting aside some money to invest for retirement. Your employer's plan will offer a dozen or so *index funds* and other *mutual funds*; some will be passive, and others will be active. *Target Date Retirement* funds are usually a blend of active and passive underlying funds designed to reduce exposure to market risks as you get closer to retirement. Again, you'll learn a lot just by *comparing fees and performance* of the various funds, but you can learn more by reading each fund's *prospectus* which is a summary of all the charges, who manages the fund and what strategy they are trying to execute to earn returns. Keep in mind that as a younger person, you have a long time before you retire so you can afford to take more risk in hopes of earning a higher return by investing in growth equities, small cap equities and even international or emerging markets equities. Fixed income, on the other hand, is typically lower risk but usually doesn't offer higher return expectations. A blended portfolio of both equities and fixed income will usually have relatively low volatility. A common split is 60% equities and 40% fixed income which serves as a *benchmark* for comparing performance if you choose more equities and less fixed income.

Now, if you've been saving for a while and you've accumulated a wide savings moat with plenty of emergency funds, you might want to *also* set up an investment account outside of your employer's retirement plan. In this case, you are looking to open a *brokerage account* with some platform, like Charles Schwab or Vanguard or Fidelity or Robinhood or any number of banks, though they *all* will try to sell you their own products, so be wary. There are also thousands of *investment advisors* who will happily sign you up as a client, do a lot of the paperwork for you and set up an account on their platform to invest. Of course, they don't do this for free, right. Advisors are compensated on a percentage basis, typically 0.25% to 1% or more annually, of the total balance of the assets you place with them. They try to *earn their fee* by placing trades in equities and mutual funds and ETFs and actively managing your portfolio to outperform some relevant benchmark like the S&P 500. But wait! Isn't this what you are learning to do by reading this book!? *YES!* You are financially literate and can do all these things on your own without paying others!

A quick note about *account types* since these can sometimes be confusing if you don't keep the terms straight in your mind. A *brokerage account* is considered a *taxable* account since the money you earn on these investments is taxable when you *realize* those gains. Short-term gains are things like dividend income, interest income and premium income from option sales and these usually are taxed during the year you earn them at your highest income tax rate. Long-term gains are usually taxed at a lower rate, but you don't *realize* the gain for at least a year. For instance, if you held KO or PEP stock for at least twelve months before selling it at a higher price, you will only owe long-term gain taxes on the difference between your sales price and purchase price. You can *defer* paying those taxes for as long as you hold the stock, even if you don't sell it for twenty or thirty years!

Brokerage accounts differ from *retirement accounts* like 401k and 403b which are *pre-tax* accounts, meaning the money in there, including gains and any employer match, has not been *taxed* yet as income by the government and *will not be taxed* until you start taking money out of that account – which you really *should not ever do* until you are required to do so or when you have no other money in savings after you retire. When you *do* start taking out the required minimum distributions during retirement, that's when you will pay the income taxes.

Remember, there is also a special kind of retirement account called a *Roth IRA* created by the government to encourage *even more* investment by individuals. This account type is funded with money that has already been taxed, but the government allows you to treat all future investment gains as *tax-free* if the money is invested for a minimum of five years or so. These accounts are so special because you can use the power of compounding for such a long time and then draw down that money in retirement *without paying more taxes*. Alternatively, you can leave this account as part of an inheritance for your kids, grandkids or good friends and *they* won't even be required to pay taxes on it! *They* will have to take the money out over the next ten years after you die, but that's a minor detail. The main thing to remember is this is a *great* way to build up the financial security you will want. And because of the power of compounding interest /

compound returns, starting *today* will make it *gobs* easier than waiting a few decades and ending up with much less in your accounts.

Brokerage Account	Taxed Current Year	Accessible Now
Traditional IRA	Taxed When Withdrawn	Accessible After 59 ½
Roth IRA	Never Taxed (Again)	Accessible After 59 ½

Most people who consider themselves investors generally stick to the equities market because they are easy to understand, they are popular, fast-moving and there is always news or companies that are familiar to them. Trading individual bonds is a little harder because you have to go through an advisor or broker/dealer who has a relationship called a prime account.

Alternatively, individuals *can* buy U.S. Treasury debt (savings bonds, bills, notes, etc.) through TreasuryDirect.gov but if you want to convert those securities to cash you must transfer them to a broker/dealer account where you will likely be charged various fees. Instead of *directly investing* in fixed income securities, most investors trade fixed income ETFs or mutual funds (which also charge fees); occasionally, brokerage platforms like Charles Schwab offer fixed income and even commodities trading capabilities, but just because you *can* do something, doesn't mean you *should*. Do your research, figure out how much things cost, start small and learn along the way.

Outside of a brokerage account, and in *very limited* cases sometimes within them or through a *self-directed IRA*, you can invest in things like real estate, LP's, LLC's and individual mortgages. These investment assets are part of the *private market* and probably don't appeal to most people because there isn't a lot of information about the underlying businesses or borrower credit risk and there are federal regulations that restrict the active trading of these interests, so they usually have no *liquidity*. Liquidity is a term that refers to the ease with which an asset can be sold and converted into spendable cash.

Any individual can form their own LP, which stands for limited partnership, or LLC, which stands for limited liability company. And if you've saved enough to help someone else buy a house, you may want to lend them the money at a generous interest rate for yourself and *lien* that property as security for repayment of the loan, an activity called *extending a mortgage* or *carrying a note*. We could spend a long time on the details of these deals but if this is an area that appeals to you, you should read one of the dozens of books about starting your own business and using the LP/LLC structure. They protect your assets while creating a vehicle or space in which to manage income and expenses, just like a big business. There are plenty of *tax advantages* to structuring your business in certain ways, so be sure and do the research and ask lots of questions from your tax advisor and others who have done it. Private equity, private lending, venture capital and angel investing are other investments addressed in a later chapter on private markets. These are interesting areas where professionals can make a lot of money very quickly, but they also accept the higher probability of losing a lot of money along the way. Pension funds and other *institutional investors* invest in these markets all the time.

To summarize: *investing* is a way to delay the spending of your money into the future when the amount you can spend has hopefully grown enormously. If you put your *capital* into an investment that earns returns for many years, and those returns are reinvested to earn additional returns, that process results in *compound returns*. Eventually, you get the original capital back, plus any increase in the value of that original amount, in addition to all the cash flow returns along the way. Buy a house for $125,000 today, rent it out for an average of $1,200 a month for twenty years and sell the house for $210,000; that's an investment. Buy a few shares of RBLX or META for $1,000 today, maybe earn some dividends along the way and sell those same shares in a few years for $35,000; that's an investment.

All the asset classes discussed above offer the potential for returns and increased value on your original purchase price; your shoes don't offer that potential, nor does that new car or cell phone or makeup or handbag or fancy meal or vacation, though that last one might be a great experience worth enjoying! Investing is a fascinating process with infinite variety; many people make a lot of money helping less financially literate folks participate in investments. If your purpose in life requires more money than you can likely earn in a modest amount of time, investing is probably the best option available to accomplish your goals. Again, money isn't the goal, but it is one of the more powerful tools you can use to get there. Hopefully, you now have some insight and interest in investing.

CHAPTER 9: NET WEALTH

"We're not worthy! We're not worthy!"
- Wayne Campbell and Garth Algar, 1992

Most people in financially literate circles will refer to a concept called *net worth*, but I prefer the slightly different formulation *net wealth*. While admittedly it is a nitpicky distinction, worth implies an equivalent value or else a character more personal than just a monetary tally. *Wealth*, in contrast, is immediately recognized as relating to an abundance of possessions or money. So how to calculate your net wealth?

(NET ASSETS) - (NET LIABILITIES) = NET WEALTH

Remember, assets are positives – you want more of these – and liabilities are negatives – you'd rather minimize these. The difference resulting from the equation (net assets) minus (net liabilities) is your net wealth. It is a snapshot taken at a point in time – just like a balance sheet – and the change from the last snapshot you took is instructive as to your ability to affect an increase or decrease in the net result. Say you start with a bank account balance of $2,500 and you have no debt: your net wealth is $2,500. A year goes by, you've earned income from a job, paid your taxes, contributed to your retirement account and spent a lot of money along the way, including the purchase of a used car for which you borrowed $9,000. You still have emergency savings of $2,500 in your bank account, your retirement plan balance is $12,000, which includes your employer's matching contribution of $2,000; the balance you still owe on your car loan is $8,500, your payments on this loan are $300 each month, and the car is probably only worth $5,500 now. Your net wealth at the end of the first year is $2,500 + $12,000 - ($8,500 - $5,500) = $11,500. Great job - that's a pretty good increase over just one year! Notice the $300/month car payments and all the money you spent don't figure into the calculation; if you sold all that junk at a yard sale, it would be a rounding error. The net wealth calculation only captures the value of assets you kept reduced by the debts you owe at the end of the period.

SNAPSHOT NOT A MOVIE

It doesn't matter how complicated your *personal balance sheet* gets throughout your life, this simple formula can be used to quickly figure out and track whether your net wealth increased or decreased. And estimated values are fine: maybe the car in the example above would've sold for $7,000 or maybe only $1,500... the stock market could have been great or sucky on the day you checked your retirement plan balance. This is just a rough estimate, a fuzzy picture, one way of measuring your wealth. It's a metric, a single number, which makes an easy target or goal to work toward.

Now, as a financially literate adult, you will know how to affect each of the moving pieces! Assets go up if you earn money and save it in the bank or invest it into a retirement or brokerage account. Liabilities increase if you blow your budget (your income is less than your expenses) and you end up assuming debt; a good budget will *help* you avoid this outcome but might not fully protect you from it. A really big savings balance will also help – remember the moat! As with the earlier car example, there is a *net* liability because the asset tied to it has some value; I generally like to pair any liabilities with the *associated* assets because it informs better decisions about the *disposition* of that asset relative to its liability – is the asset generating a better return than it costs me to *carry* it? Or is the asset likely to increase in value so it will eventually be worth more than it cost me, including all interest expense along the way?

Tracking your balance sheet or net wealth over a long period of time is a great way to make a fun game out of your *money life* as compared to your social life or your family life or your professional life. You can always estimate your net wealth and decide how to best use it to help you achieve your purpose in life. Most people do not set their purpose in life equal to working a job for 50 years and then retiring on the beach to read books and catch skin cancer! The job is just a tool to make money; money is just a tool to create security and help you achieve your aspirational goals. This book describes the fundamental things you can do to maximize the utility of that money and grow your net wealth balance as quickly as possible so you can get on with the *important* things in your life! A job is not the most important thing, but it sure takes up a lot of time, right? So, recognize how a growing net wealth balance can help you reduce that time suck and increase the amount of time you spend pursuing your purpose!

ESCAPING THE RAT RACE♪

Earning money is the fastest way to increase your balance of money – at least early in your career. Welcome to the *rat race*! You don't start with much, you earn a lot and hopefully save a lot, but *you* are doing all the work to increase your cash pile. Later, as you start investing, your *capital* gets to work for you – compound interest, compound returns, increasing asset values. At some point, you could set a goal for yourself to have *more* dividends and interest *income* from your *investments* than you *make from your job's salary*. This is hard because you probably get paid more each year you work since you are more valuable to your employer with more experience, but earning more from investment income is a totally achievable goal! Play with your compound interest table and find that point where *interest* or *return* on a monthly basis exceeds your current salary. How can you get that month to happen earlier? By *contributing* more or earning a *higher return*. How can you contribute more? By increasing your earnings or lowering your expenses, by paying off debt and using that payment amount to increase contributions.

By the way, any time your earnings increase, the target monthly amount gets higher which works in the opposite direction of your goal for a while. Catch 22? Not really, because you can always tell yourself your real goal is some fixed amount per month rather than an ever-increasing salary amount. It's a game, your game! You get to make all the rules! If you play *this* game rather than run in the *rat race*, your goal is to have enough capital earning enough of a monthly cash return that you don't have to work any longer. Some people call that retirement, and they don't get there until they are 60, 65 or maybe never. I call the decision to not work any longer *freedom*. If, according to Einstein, debt enslaves a productive society then accumulating enough capital which earns more than all your expenses should be considered freedom!

Financially literate people understand the tools discussed in this book and how to use these tools to gain their freedom. Some folks figure out how to do it very quickly – entrepreneurship is one of those ways, but not without a lot of risks along the way. Some folks just get super lucky and make numerous wise investments or get blessed with game show winnings, a lottery or inheritance. Many other folks – including me! – take a slower, methodical approach through education and a rewarding career... and *still* manage to meet their goals by diligently spending less than they earn, saving and investing in prudent ways, seldom deviating from their budget, and always trying to increase their knowledge and apply it wisely. The path you take is less important than your determination to achieve your goals. I hope this text has given you enough of a grounding in the important tools you will need to make strides toward your goals using money rather than allowing money to use you. Again, please don't worship money, it is not the goal – it is just a tool to help you achieve your purpose.

CHAPTER 10: MACRO ECONOMICS

This last section of four chapters is less focused on *you*, the individual, or what *you* can do to achieve your goals in life. Instead, this chapter provides some broad context and insights into the *environment* which affects *all* financial activity; the last three chapters touch on each of the major asset classes available to investors. There are literally hundreds of books written in much more detail about economics and investing in bond markets, stock markets and private markets.   Consider these next chapters as mere introductions to hopefully serve as a launch pad for exploring more and figuring out how to invest your money more effectively. Who knows? You may even find an area that ignites a passion in you to learn everything about that topic and you could create a whole new business to feed that passion! Welcome to a new purpose in life!

Alas, now we begin with the *dismal science*... I know, not very encouraging as far as a new purpose in life goes, eh? Economics is the term used to describe the *discipline* or study of the economy. Not helpful: what's an economy? The economy is the environment in which businesses buy and sell the products that get manufactured, and in which people are paid or spend money for the services they provide.   Governments provide a medium of exchange, called currency, which is used to complete transactions and determine values. They also set the interest rates at which big pools of money can be borrowed or lent out to facilitate transactions.

Macro-economics ("big") deals with matters of global influence and importance – things like interest rates, inflation, demographics, production and trade around the world, and logistics security – whereas micro-economics ("small") is focused on *individual* transactions in the context of supply and demand, utility and what drives individuals' decisions to buy or sell things. For now, let's just focus on the big picture – things that affect global markets and might influence the performance of your investments and opportunities for returns. You can take micro-economics in college if you like math and graphs.

INTEREST RATES AND INFLATION

In the U.S. the Federal Reserve System, or The Fed, is responsible for a few big things, but the two that get the most attention are *inflation* and *employment levels*. The Fed is tasked with monitoring the rate of increase in the prices of things, a *basket of goods and services,* to ensure people can reasonably expect the prices today are likely to be close to the prices they'll pay tomorrow. This is called *price stability* which eases the fear "if I don't buy this today, I may not be able to afford it tomorrow" and helps the ongoing process of the economy to run smoothly. If prices varied wildly, we would focus all our time trying to decide what we needed and how much of it we could afford; money would never be spent wisely because we wouldn't be able to budget well. Sucks when one of your best tools for managing money – the budget – doesn't work because you never know what things will cost in the near future! So, the Fed tries to make sure inflation is reasonably well controlled with their target somewhere around 2% annually.

Alas, the Fed can't tell businesses to raise their prices by only 2% every year; besides, prices for *some* things decline over time, like computers or TV's or t-shirts. But they *can* make it more expensive for companies to borrow and more costly for people to spend their money rather than save it. These are called decision incentives, and the Fed controls a very powerful lever over incentives – the short-term interest rate, also called the *Fed Funds Rate*. If the Fed funds rate is low, say 1%, then all other debts that *reference* that rate will also be low; if the Fed's rate is high, say 5%, then all that other debt that references the Fed rate will also be about four percentage points higher. That makes a huge difference when you borrow billions of dollars to run a business! It also hurts when you try to buy a home with an 80% loan-to-value on a $250,000 house (you can create an amortization table now and see what the difference is in monthly payments and interest expense over time). Historically, the Fed has *raised rates* whenever inflation or credit activity increases too quickly according to their models; they have historically *lowered rates* whenever *unemployment* is high or rising faster than they want. The idea is to keep as many people employed so they can spend money but not spend so much money that producers decide they should raise prices too quickly. Also, if everybody is employed, they can demand higher wages, which leads to more spending, and further pushes prices for everything higher. So, the Fed funds rate is like an accelerator and a brake on inflation by way of influencing the economy through the price (i.e., cost or interest rate) of money.

With respect to investments, a higher Fed funds rate raises the cost of debt. If you are a borrower, this is bad, but if you are a saver and a lender, this is great! Banks peg their savings rates to the Fed funds rate, depending on whether they have plenty of customers or if they need more capital to invest; remember, they have to attract your capital so they can lend it at a higher interest rate to their borrowers. If you are investing in fixed income securities, the interest rate at which you can now lend to new borrowers – governments, companies and individuals – is higher meaning you will get paid more for every dollar you lend for as long as it is outstanding. Another trick to keep in mind is borrowing when interest rates are low and leaving that "cheap" debt outstanding for a long time, as with a thirty-year mortgage, because it allows you to potentially invest more money in the future when interest rates are higher. In these cases, you are like a bank, earning a spread between your *higher* lending rate and your *lower* borrowing rate.

One last point on inflation: there are examples in history when inflation gets out of hand; those are fascinating case studies to read about and think about. Inflation reduces the *spending power* of money that you earn because the things you need to buy will be more expensive. So, you demand higher pay from your employer, and they have to raise their prices for the things you make or the services you provide, and things can *spiral* out of control. If you buy the same basket of groceries that cost $120 today but only cost $100 last week, the spending power of your money is weaker. On the other hand, think about that fixed rate, thirty-year home mortgage: your payment amount hasn't changed and if you get that raise to cover the inflated cost of your grocery basket, you probably have more money to pay that mortgage, too. So, inflation works to erode the value of the money you earn but also, somewhat helpfully, erodes the value of the debt you carry because, in theory, it is easier to pay off that debt with *inflated* dollars. It's a bit of a mind-bender, but if you think about it long enough, you'll see why the Fed is focused on maintaining price stability and full employment.

DEBT AND DEMOGRAPHICS

Global debt is as big picture as it gets: governments around the world are constantly short of cash to support the many spending programs they create to keep their politicians in power. Government borrowing is "safe" for investing because they can *levy taxes* on the citizens and use that tax money to pay off the debt. Of course, it would be smarter if they collected (fewer) taxes and invested them wisely in advance of big spending projects; that way they wouldn't have to pay interest on debt. But politicians are not known for being financially literate. Maybe *you* should become a politician after implementing the lessons you've learned in this book... then give me a tax break, would ya? So, governments borrow tons of money, usually from other governments because the amounts are so huge, but individuals can participate, too. It makes some sense because it's very rare for a government to *default* on their debt, though it has happened plenty of times in the past. The U.S. government is considered a sterling credit with almost zero probability of defaulting, so the shortest-term debt that has the lowest interest rate is called a *risk-free rate* and usually refers to Treasury bills with only a few weeks or months before they mature. Almost every other debt that is created by banks and businesses extending credit is a *spread* over that risk free rate to compensate the lender for various risks of getting paid back in full, including all interest charges.

Demographics refers to the characteristics of a *population* and the various *classes* of people within that population. Population in this context usually refers to the number of people in a country or state; the classes are typically categorized into age groups, or ethnic groups, or credit scores, or political party affiliation, etc. There are some fascinating books that study the dynamics of global economies – those of each country and as blocs of countries compared to others –

with respect to their underlying *demographics*. You should read at least one of those books. At a high level, though, if a country is growing its population, either through natural birth rates or immigration, then there are more people to produce, consume, build, create... and tax. This is a great characteristic for a country to have as long as everyone is trying to be productive; less helpful if people are not working and just being lazy, or worse, stealing and breaking things that others have bought or built. Unfortunately, many countries across Europe and Asia do not have healthy demographics: they are either shrinking or growing older (as a population, not just the individuals) because they do not have a high enough birthrate relative to the speed with which people are dying, or because they are experiencing *emigration* – the opposite of immigration. It can be doubly bad if emigration is also *brain drain,* meaning the brightest and most productive of that country's citizens are choosing to leave. The U.S. has been a beneficiary of other countries' brain drain troubles despite its natural birthrate failing to keep up with the pace at which our country's people are aging and dying. Latin America and some countries in Africa still have relatively high birthrates, so they aren't shrinking as quickly as they otherwise could, but many of those countries have very low economic productivity. Demographics are super important for government policy and affect markets by adding or subtracting the number of productive people that could be potential consumers or suppliers of labor or other resources.

Think about this potential problem: a country borrowed billions and billions to build infrastructure and castle walls and apartments for its millions of citizens, but now those citizens do not have as many babies as they used to, and in fact, many of their university professors and entrepreneurs decide to move their families to other countries because the taxes they pay are so high in order to pay off that debt. This happens a lot. People make choices based on their personal incentives but may be constrained by various laws. China is an interesting case study because its economy has grown so quickly since the mid-20th century; India is amazing, too, because they have undergone so much change in a short amount of time for such a large and diverse population; Japan is another fascinating example of a troubling demographic picture and restrictive immigration laws; Russia is a different kind of crazy with immense separation between the *haves* and the *have nots*. The entire continent of Africa is mystifying and terrifying and yet holds such promise for a better demographic future, if only... a lot of things could be different.

PRODUCTION AND TRADE

A global perspective leads to some expansive thoughts. Consider the things you own and where those things were made. Services maybe aren't as interesting because you can only go so far to buy dinner at a restaurant or have someone come clean your home or repair your car. But where did your car get manufactured? Your cell phone? Your shoes? After World War II a lot of decisions were made and patterns got locked-in such that many things made in many different countries now find a global market of buyers, though none so prolific as the U.S. Even U.S. companies that used to make things here in the U.S. found ways to lower costs by moving *production* to other countries with lower labor costs. It was even cheap enough to send finished products back to the U.S. and *still* charge lower prices than by making those things here. This is called the *globalization of manufacturing and trade*. Products now move all over the world, prices are lower for everything, and willing buyers exist primarily in the U.S. and Europe but also in Latin America and other Asian countries. Lowering the cost of goods made those goods accessible to more people so *everyone* in the world benefitted in some way or another and *most* of those people became consumers to some degree. You should read books about globalization and consider what happens if that supportive environment for investment changes. Where will new investment opportunities arise? What kinds of businesses would be needed and where would they be located? What happens if costs for *things* increase and people stop buying so much stuff?

ECONOMIC DISRUPTION

The point here is that nothing stays the same and globalization has been such a huge influence for so long, we tend not to think about it. In the world of investing, everything can hum along smoothly for many years, everybody makes money, but *in an instant*, some *disruption* upturns the apple cart: markets sell off quickly, prices of equities collapse, and a credit crisis makes borrowing prohibitively expensive, even for the highest quality borrowers.

Investing relies critically on views about possible futures, forecasting possibilities, and evaluating which industries and companies or which debt positions will be winners... and which ones will be losers. It is more important to avoid losers – those investments that eventually turn out to be worthless – than to pick the one company that shoots the lights out and experiences huge gains in their equity price. In a global context, wars are *disruptive* because everyone nearby, including other countries, must scramble to minimize their losses or otherwise find new sources for the things they previously bought from the countries in conflict. *Pandemics* are obviously disruptive as Covid-19 showed us: plenty of companies and industries, like real estate, hotels and restaurants, suffered and went bankrupt, while others like ZM, AMZN, NFLX, MRNA and LULU enjoyed record earnings and huge stock price gains. The world changed abruptly and suddenly there were new investment opportunities while other investments went sour.

As you invest more, investigate more and always think in terms of scenarios, alternate universes where things change in a big way and end up very different than they are today. This disciplined approach can steer you away from blind mistakes, can help protect your wealth and keep you on the path to achieving your purpose. It's also fun, enlightening and makes for great party conversation! If you're in to that kind of thing... parties, I mean. And conversation.

CHAPTER 11: THE FIXED INCOME MARKETS

The fixed income markets encompass a host of *issuers* or borrowers. The market is staggeringly huge on a global scale. It's easy to understand why, just consider banks: they are borrowing from depositors, who are saving a little money, and then lend that same money to other borrowers like businesses, who in turn may be lending to consumers, extending them credit to buy their merchandise. That same consumer may already owe the bank on a car loan and a mortgage! Debt can have a multiplier effect on the economy which means one dollar borrowed and spent somewhere probably gets lent out again and spent again and again. There are plenty of technical books on this subject called velocity of money and money supply which affects government monetary policy and everything in the financial markets. Thus, understanding the fixed income markets is critical. Especially if you want to invest in them, which I suggest is a good thing.

TREASURIES AND OTHER SOVEREIGN DEBT
U.S. Treasuries – and other sovereign government debt – is probably the largest class of debt traded in the fixed income market. It totals *trillions of dollars* in outstanding obligations and hundreds of billions of that total is traded, bought and sold, every day. Treasuries, and all other debts for that matter, are borrowed for specific periods of time called a *term* or *tenor* and when the term is over, the bond or debt is considered to have *matured,* and the principal must be repaid. Debt borrowed for one day is called *overnight* and they are charged

the Fed Funds Rate: only member banks of the Federal Reserve get to participate here. Next in line are short-term Treasury *bills* (T-bills, not those guys from Buffalo) and they are typically issued with terms to maturity of four weeks up to one year. They are sold at a discount of something like $1 to *face value or par* of $1,000 and that discount is what you earn as "interest" when you get paid back. Treasury *notes* are issued with maturity dates of 2, 3, 5, 7 and 10 years and they pay a stated, annualized, fixed interest rate every six months (i.e., a 6%, $1,000 note might pay $30 on June 15 and $30 on December 15 and when it matures you will get $1,030 back). The longest U.S. Treasuries are called *bonds* and they come in 20-year and 30-year varieties but work the same way notes do. Some countries offer 50- or even 100-year bonds! For convenience, most debts are called bonds.

SECONDARY DEBT TRADING

You can buy a bond when it is originally *issued* by the borrower and depending on supply and demand, you might be able to buy $1,000 worth of bonds for only $990 or even less and thus earn a higher return than the interest rate stated on the bond. Occasionally investors will pay even more than the face amount of the bond. Wait, what!? Why would you pay more? Well, it happens, and the end result is you make a little lower return than that stated interest rate on the bond if you do this. We saw this happen a lot during the Global Financial Crisis and during the early stages of Covid-19 when folks thought the world was about to end. It didn't and those people probably lost a little money when they later sold the bond for less or turned it in at maturity and got only the face amount of the bond.

Now, nobody said you have to hold a bond until it matures. Depending on the direction and movement of interest rates, today's price of any bond you bought could go up or down, sometimes by quite a bit. The fixed income markets are constantly trying to adjust for all the various *risk factors* that people believe affect the interest rate that should be earned for holding that *promise to pay* which is all a *bond* stands for, like "my word is my bond... James Bond." Fixed income investors care less about your word and more about your creditworthiness, your ability and willingness to pay them back. Higher risk credits must pay higher interest rates. A longer time to maturity carries a higher risk that something will go wrong before maturity and the bond owner might not get their principal paid back. If all the people of a country leave and there are no taxes to collect, the government might just print a bunch of worthless currency to pay back their bonds, so investors dump them for any price before they get stuck with a bunch of worthless paper. Think Weimar Republic pre-World War II or Zimbabwe's $100 trillion dollar bill... in 2023! "Say, like what you've done with the place... nice wallpaper! Bet it cost more to print all those bills than they are worth!" Where was I... Bonds, both government and corporate, trade all the time in what's known as the *secondary market*. For individual investors platforms like Charles Schwab, Fidelity, Interactive Brokers, SoFi, etc. offer brokerage accounts that allow trading in both equities and fixed income securities.

CORPORATE DEBT

Corporate debt, bonds issued by companies, is traded in a way that is similar to Treasuries but they usually have more kinds of debt, with varying *priorities,* called *seniority,* and other features that either enhance security – the likelihood of getting paid all the interest and principal down the road – or adjust the interest rate over time, called floating rate debt. This happens because companies usually have an idea how they want to use the debt and investors want to be certain of getting that money back. It is a negotiated process, led by bankers and sophisticated financiers who are all trying to get the best deal for themselves. The catch: that deal depends on the *prevailing interest rate environment* and other business conditions. If the debt is priced too high (i.e., the interest rate is too low), there may not be enough buyers of the debt; alternatively, if the debt is priced too low (i.e., interest rate or other terms are very attractive for the lenders), the issue could be *oversubscribed* and the buyers of the debt might be willing to pay more than face value to get some of those issues.

Corporate debt issues are usually classified in terms of creditworthiness *rated* by various agencies who do that kind of thing:

- Investment grade debt is "very likely to repay all principal and interest,"
- Non-investment grade issues have the "potential for some loss of capital or income" before maturity.

Another term for sub-non-investment grade debt is high yield or junk bonds. Some companies are stuck plying their trade in risky businesses and so lenders make them pay a higher interest rate; but if those businesses succeed and they generate enough sales and profits to cover that interest, everyone makes money.

SECURITIZED DEBT

Consider those car loans and mortgages and credit card balances we explored in earlier chapters. Would you believe those companies that financed your purchase just turned around and stapled your *promise to pay* along with 1,000 other borrowers of the same kind of debt and sold that big stack to other buyers/lenders? Yep. Here's what happens... all the time. For instance, when you buy something from a store using your credit card, the card issuer pays the merchant (after taking their fee) and you are obligated to pay back the card issuer, something like 5% of your outstanding balance every month. Assume they do this for 1,000 people, ending up with a combined balance of $10 million, about $10,000 of credit card debt per person.

Since you are now financially literate, you're shaking your head in horror because with your quick math skills you just realized each person is paying $200 *per month* in interest at 24% annualized...

The card issuers find bankers who sell that stack of promises – and the $200,000 monthly interest income – to institutional investors, like pension funds and sovereign wealth funds and foundations and college endowments and high net worth individuals. The card company has now *securitized* those 1,000 debts into a bond that pays interest and *amortizes* the principal balance over time as the people pay off their cards. Once they sell that bond to investors, they have more money to extend credit to another 1,000 consumers and earn more fees and interest. Rinse and repeat!

The same thing happens with your car loans and your home mortgages which are *securitized* with thousands of other similar notes then sliced into different *tranches* of debt with varying characteristics. Those tranches are sold to hundreds of other investors who assume very specific risks they are comfortable bearing in exchange for earning a return they believe is fair and appropriate. Sometimes all your fixed rate debt gets converted into floating rate tranches that pay in completely different currencies! It's absolutely mind-boggling, but it's all possible *and profitable*! because very financially literate people have figured out how to make money using other people's debt and trading that debt in fixed income markets around the world.

OTHER KINDS OF DEBT

Certificates of deposit (CD's), also called *time deposits*, are offered by banks so they know how long they can use your money in exchange for slightly higher interest than a savings account. Your money is "locked up" for that period of time but you can still get it in an emergency by paying a penalty and forgoing the interest you would have otherwise earned. Money market funds are just mutual funds that invest in short-maturity *paper* and other government obligations, or even municipal debt. Think of CD's and money market funds as low risk, low return savings accounts rather than investments; also, they are considered *less liquid* than a savings account because you are penalized for accessing the money in a CD and it takes a day to get the money market funds. Longer dated notes and bonds come with a little more risk, mostly just a discount rate applied for the length of time until maturity if associated with Treasuries, or a few other risks if dealing with a state or municipal bond, but those kinds of securities tend to offer a slightly better interest rate as a return on your investment. And some state and local bonds even have special tax advantages that are attractive to high income earners wishing to minimize their tax burden while still earning a good return. Debt markets are huge and relatively liquid, so if you end up owning some, you should be able to sell it into the market for cash without taking a big price discount, but it's still more costly to trade than equities.

CHAPTER 12: THE EQUITY MARKETS

For a much more *volatile* ride, let's check out the stock market! Equities, as we've already discussed in earlier chapters, represent ownership in a business. First, we should understand what a business really is.

<u>BUSINESS STRUCTURE</u>

There's a great little book called *The Company: A Short History of a Revolutionary Idea* that offers an eye-opening history of businesses and how they came to be known as *joint-stock corporations* owned by hundreds or thousands of individuals. Despite no connection with the business itself, individual investors used their capital to buy partial ownership "shares" which could then be sold and bought again in public markets. It doesn't really matter who owns a company if you have professional managers running it day-to-day.

Think of a business as a kind of room in which a bunch of different activity takes place: inputs like raw materials/supplies, technology, people and capital come in; things get done inside the room; and products or services get sent out to customers and clients who pay money back into the business which pays that money out to lenders, owners and suppliers for more resources to keep the cycle going. That's all a business is. Some businesses are tiny: a guy with a lawnmower and a smile turns 50 neighbors into customers and that's his business. Other companies are so large that they span the globe with offices, employ hundreds of thousands of employees, churn billions of dollars every week and make more money in profits each month for its owners than some *countries* make in an entire year. Most big U.S. businesses are corporations, meaning they have *incorporated* or made themselves a legal entity, usually in the state of Delaware, and have similar rights as those of a physical person. Imagine iRobot headquartered in Bedford, MA saying, "Oh wow! I'm a real boy!" Smaller businesses often use a different legal structure called a Limited Liability Corporation which can be owned by numerous *shareholders*, the same idea underlying the concept of a joint-stock corporation. It's a fancy way of saying "a bunch of people put their capital together and now own this room, or *shell,* of an entity that makes and does things in return for income."

Limited Partnerships work slightly differently, but the same idea applies: more than one person combines their capital and expertise to share the risk of operating a business and making profits. An S-Corp, or *sole proprietorship*, is a more closely-held form of business, usually within a single family or by one individual, but these can also be very large businesses... they just don't usually have very many owners. There are all sorts of books written about how to use corporations as *tax shields* and they are very instructive as to why companies choose the various forms they do. Bottom line: businesses exist to make a profit for their owners and minimizing taxes is a fundamental part of maximizing the returns on the capital invested by owners.

FINANCIAL STATEMENTS

A publicly traded company, one that goes through the complexity of listing shares of ownership on one of the many stock exchanges around the world, are *regulated* here in the U.S. by the Securities and Exchange Commission (SEC) and must follow various rules of the exchanges to provide financial transparency to its owners. The primary mechanism for this is *financial statements* and *disclosures*. You shouldn't be surprised by the format of financial statements a company must produce because they are basically the same thing this book already covered!

Financial statements have a *balance sheet* listing all the company's *assets* and all its *liabilities*, as well as something called *shareholder's equity* which is conceptually similar to *net wealth* from earlier. If you add up all liabilities and all the owner's equity it must total the same value as all assets; it is a snapshot at one point in time, usually the end of a calendar quarter or year.

The *income statement* shows all the income and expenses that were incurred during a given period, again, usually one calendar quarter or year. The total income can be positive, even after taxes and payment of interest on debt, or it might occasionally be negative, but you hope that doesn't last too long or else the company can go bankrupt or be forced to raise more money from its existing owners, or possibly bring in new owners. A standard reference point for most income statements is something called Earnings Before Interest, Taxes, Depreciation, and Amortization (EBITDA) because that is the *effective earnings* that shareholders extrapolate into the future as a way of estimating their future returns on investing in the company.

The last financial statement element is the *cash flow* statement, which captures the same information as our budget template: what cash did you make and where did you spend, save or invest it? For companies these are called *cash flow from operations* (which you hope is positive and growing), *cash flow from investing* (which is often negative as the business invests in new machines, technology or other businesses), and *cash flow from financing* (which can be positive if the company just borrowed a lot of money or raised new equity capital; alternatively, it can be negative if the company paid down debt or bought its own shares in the open market or paid its shareholders dividends).

Financial statements are used by *financial analysts* to evaluate the merits of investing in companies and forecast how quickly those companies will *grow* or *burn cash*. Financial statements help analysts decide whether to invest more capital in the company's equity or debt. There is a very deep knowledge base and rigorous study required to do *financial statement analysis* well. I won't belabor it here but check out the Chartered Financial Analyst program and you'll discover how fascinating and intellectually rewarding this profession can be.

INDEX CONSTRUCTION AND PERFORMANCE
To this point, we've touched on what a business is and why someone might want to own a piece of it and then we skimmed the financial statements that companies produce so its owners know what's going on. You can buy and sell individual companies in your brokerage account, or you can hold an entire, well-balanced

collection of companies through ETFs or mutual funds. Many of these funds just track well-defined *indexes,* like NASDAQ 100, S&P 500 or Dow Jones Industrial Average, which you can also buy at a very low cost. But what differences are indexes trying to capture or represent? NASDAQ 100 is often cited as a *bellwether* for technology companies because many of the biggest and most well-known tech companies chose to list their shares on that exchange. The S&P 500 tries to capture a representative sample of the entire U.S. economy by allocating a small percentage to each of 500 different companies, regardless of the exchange on which they are listed. The publisher of the S&P 500 index weights the holdings within and across each sector of the economy in a way they believe reflects economic activity.

SECTOR- AND INDUSTRY WEIGHTS WITHIN THE S&P 500 INDEX

Communication Services	10.2
Interactive Media & Services	46.1
Integrated Telecommunication Services	20.5
Movies & Entertainment	16.7
Cable & Satellite	10.0
Interactive Home Entertainment	3.4
Broadcasting	1.3
Advertising	1.1
Alternative Carriers	0.7
Publishing & Printing	0.3

Consumer Discretionary	9.9
Internet & Direct Marketing Retail	35.1
Home Improvement Retail	12.9
Restaurants	12.8
Apparel Retail	4.9
Hotels, Resorts & Cruise Lines	4.7
Footwear	4.5
General Merchandise Stores	4.0
Automobile Manufacturers	3.6
Automotive Retail	3.4
Apparel, Accessories & Luxury Goods	3.0
Specialty Stores	1.6
Homebuilding	1.5
Department Stores	1.2
Auto Parts & Equipment	1.1
Distributors	1.1
Casinos & Gaming	1.0
Leisure Products	0.6
Computer & Electronics Retail	0.6
Home Furnishings	0.6
Housewares & Specialties	0.4
Consumer Electronics	0.4
Household Appliances	0.3
Motorcycle Manufacturers	0.3
Specialized Consumer Services	0.3
Tires & Rubber	0.2

Materials	2.7
Diversified Chemicals	23.1
Specialty Chemicals	22.2
Industrial Gases	21.3
Paper Packaging	8.1
Fertilizers & Agricultura Chemicals	5.2
Commodity Chemicals	4.5
Construction Materials	4.1
Gold	3.2
Steel	2.9
Metal & Glass Containers	2.7
Copper	2.6

Consumer Staples	7.4
Soft Drinks	23.0
Household Products	22.8
HyperMarkets & Super Centers	14.2
Packaged Foods & Meats	14.2
Tobacco	12.7
Drug Retail	3.5
Distillers & Vintners	2.3
Personal Products	2.0
Food Distributors	1.9
Agricultural Products	1.5
Food Retail	1.4
Brewers	0.7

Energy	5.3
Integrated Oil & Gas	48.7
Exploration & Production	24.3
Refining & Marketing	10.4
Equipment & Services	9.3
Storage & Transportation	6.9
Drilling	0.5

Financials	13.3
Diversified Banks	33.7
Multi-Sector Holdings	14.4
Regional Banks	8.4
Financial Exchanges & Data	7.6
Asset Management Custody Banks	6.8
Investment Banking & Brokerage	6.4
Property & Casualty Insurance	6.0
Life & Health Insurance	5.3
Consumer Finance	4.9
Insurance Brokers	3.9
Multi-line Insurance	2.4
Reinsurance	0.3

Real Estate	3.0
Specialized REITs	40.3
Retail REITs	16.1
Residential REITs	14.9
Health Care REITs	9.7
Office REITs	7.6
Industrial REITs	7.4
Real Estate Services	2.0
Hotel & Resort REITs	2.0

Utilities	3.4
Electric Utilities	62.0
Multi-Utilities	32.7
Independent Power Producers Traders	3.0
Water Utilities	2.3

Health Care	15.5
Pharmaceuticals	33.6
Health Care Equipment	20.8
Biotechnology	16.9
Managed Health Care	11.7
Life Sciences Services	6.5
Health Care Services	5.8
Health Care Distributors	1.8
Health Care Facilities	1.3
Health Care Supplies	1.1
Health Care Technology	0.5

Industrials	9.2
Aerospace & Defense	27.0
Industrial Conglomerates	15.7
Railroads	10.5
Industrial Machinery	8.3
Air Freight & Logistics	6.7
Construction Machinery Heavy Trucks	5.9
Electrical Componen & Equipment	5.2
Airlines	4.9
Environmental & Facilities Services	2.9
Building Products	2.9
Research & Consulting Services	2.8
Agricultural & Farm Machinery	2.5
Trading Companies & Distributor	1.9
Diversified Support Services	1.3
Construction & Engineering	0.8
Trucking	0.4
Human Resource Employer Services	0.4

Information Technology	20.1
Systems Software	22.6
Technology Hardware, Storage Peripherals	19.1
Data Processing Outsource Services	17.1
Semiconductors	17.1
Application Software	8.1
IT Consulting Other Services	6.1
Communications Equipment	5.7
Semiconductor Equipment	1.6
Electronic Components	1.2
Electronic Manufactu Services	0.7
Internet Services & Infrastructu	0.6
Electronic Equipment & Instrument	0.4

All values in percent terms

Since economic activity changes over time, the index evolves over time to accommodate and adjusts the percentage allocation to those largest companies in each sector. A free website called finviz.com offers an excellent graphical representation of this concept reflecting each company's weight in the index (size of the company's box) grouped by their industry sector, and relative daily return (color of their box: greens for positive and reds for negative). It is hours of mindless entertainment to watch the colors change throughout the trading day! Check it out!

TECHNOLOGY
SOFTWARE - INFRASTRUCTURE
MSFT
-0.10%
ORCL
+0.20%
ADBE
-0.33%
SEMICONDUCTORS
NVDA
-0.53%
AVGO
-0.62%
AMD
-0.76%
QCOM
-1.71%
TXN
-1.16%
MU
-2.30%
INTC
-1.52%
ADI
-0.56%
CONSUMER ELECTRONICS
AAPL
-1.05%
SOFTWARE - APPLICATI
CRM
-0.01%
UBER
-1.16%
NOW
-0.80%
INTU
-1.40%
AMAT
-2.70%
KLAC
INFORMATION
ACN
-0.22%
IBM
-0.10%
CSCO
-0.15%
COMMUNICATION SERVICES
INTERNET CONTENT & INFORMATION
GOOG
-2.31%
META
-0.14%
TELECOM SERVICES
TMUS
-0.69%
VZ
T
+1.07%
CMCSA
+0.14%
ENTERTAINMENT
DIS
+0.89%
NFLX
-0.96%
CONSUMER CYCLICAL
INTERNET RETAIL
AMZN
+0.11%
AUTO MANUFAC
TSLA
+1.45%
HOME IMPROVE
HD
+0.31%
RESTAURANTS
MCD
+0.54%
SBUX
-1.23%
TRAVELS
BKNG
CONSUMER DEFENSI
DISCOUNT STORES
WMT
+0.14%
COST
+0.54%
HOUSEHOLD
PG
+0.27%
BEVERAGES
KO
-0.15%
PEP
-0.68%
TOBACCO
PM
HEALTHCARE
DRUG MANUFACTURERS - GENERAL
LLY
-1.17%
JNJ
-0.01%
MRK
-0.75%
ABBV
-0.73%
PFE
+1.08%
HEALTHCARE PLANS
UNH
-4.92%
DIAGNOSTICS & RESEARC
TMO
+0.70%
DHR
0.00%
MEDICAL DEVICES
SYK
-0.60%
BSX
-0.61%
ABT
+0.14%
MDT
-0.41%
INDUSTRIALS
SPECIALTY INDUST
GE
ETN
+1.16%
AEROSPACE &
BA
-2.27%
RTX
-0.35%
FARM &
CAT
+0.47%
INTEGRATED
UPS
-0.57%
RAILROA
UNP
+0.55%
REAL ESTAT
ENERGY
OIL & GAS INTEGRATED
XOM
+0.36%
CVX
0.00%
OIL & GAS E
COP
UTILITIES
UTILITIES - REGUL
NEE
-0.99%
BASIC MATERIAL
SPECIALTY
LIN
FINANCIAL
CREDIT SERVICES
V
+0.85%
MA
+0.50%
AXP
+0.12%
BANKS - DIVERSI
JPM
+0.54%
BAC
+0.06%
WFC
+0.06%
INSURANCE - DIVERSIFI
BRK-B
+0.83%
ASSET MANAGE
BX
BLK
CAPITAL MAR
MS
GS
+0.54%
FINANCIAL DATA & ST
SPGI
ICE
CME
-3%
-2%
-1%
0%
+1%
+2%
+3%

Wrapping up with the Dow Jones Industrial Average, it was originally intended as a broad economy bellwether but that was in the late 19th and early 20th century when *industrial* companies made up the lion's share of the market. Today, industrial companies make up a far smaller percentage of economic activity, but they are all still important and the thirty names in this index are easily recognizable.

Components of the Dow Jones Industrial Average					
Company	Symbol	Weight	Company	Symbol	Weight
Unitedhealth Group Inc	UNH	8.63%	Apple Inc	AAPL	3.07%
Microsoft Corp	MSFT	6.85%	Amazon.com Inc	AMZN	2.92%
Goldman Sachs Group Inc	GS	6.52%	Johnson & Johnson	JNJ	2.70%
Home Depot Inc	HD	6.31%	Procter & Gamble Co	PG	2.68%
Caterpillar Inc	CAT	5.50%	Chevron Corp	CVX	2.56%
Salesforce Inc	CRM	5.03%	Merck & Co. Inc.	MRK	2.17%
Mcdonald S Corp	MCD	4.94%	Walt Disney Co	DIS	1.84%
Visa Inc Class A Shares	V	4.76%	Nike Inc Cl B	NKE	1.77%
Amgen Inc	AMGN	4.68%	3m Co	MMM	1.55%
Travelers Cos Inc	TRV	3.73%	Coca Cola Co	KO	1.01%
American Express Co	AXP	3.66%	Walmart Inc	WMT	1.00%
Boeing Co	BA	3.38%	Dow Inc	DOW	0.93%
Honeywell Int'l Inc	HON	3.33%	Cisco Systems Inc	CSCO	0.81%
IBM Corp	IBM	3.11%	Intel Corp	INTC	0.72%
Jpmorgan Chase & Co	JPM	3.08%	Verizon Commun. Inc.	VZ	0.67%

SECTORS AND CAPITALIZATION

Other indexes try to capture different characteristics so investors can gauge how different kinds of businesses are doing. Businesses are organized by the kind of industry or sector they are in, so you might find CSX in the railroad category because it's, well, a railroad company and you would expect to find JPM in the financial sector because it's a big bank. TSLA could legitimately be considered a technology company but for now it is categorized as an auto manufacturer which is a subset of consumer cyclicals. These are all just short-hand ways of thinking about the kinds of businesses these companies operate, but it allows investors to make investments in a very targeted way if they develop an informed view as to the future of one industry or sector versus another.

Remember long-short[♪] investing? Here's an application of that: if you believe technology is going to perform well and all companies in that *space* are going to the *moooon*, baby! but you believe utilities are going to *crater* (no pun intended... well, maybe a little intentional), you might buy a technology index long (or even better, a levered ETF on some technology subsector) and sell a utilities index short (or just find an inverse ETF for the utilities sector since it would be designed to go up in price when the sector falls in value). This is easier than picking which one or two or three of all those companies to buy; just buy and sell them all since the entire category tends to move in tandem.

Well, that's the theory anyway. You should watch the markets, make some predictions and figure out *paper trades* pretending you put real money to work, then monitor your "investment" until you believe the thesis has played out or isn't going to and then *close out* your imaginary trade. How'd you do? Make a million? Go bust? Doesn't matter cuz it wasn't real money, but that's how you build an understanding of market structure and trading flow; gain confidence along with knowledge.

Rather than refer to sectors, another way to think of stock categories is called *capitalization* and no, it doesn't refer to the reason tickers are in ALL-CAPS! Large-cap companies typically have at least a $10 billion market capitalization: a company with one billion trading shares and a $10 billion capitalization is priced at $10 per share. These companies are big and historically show slower and slower growth in their earnings as they get bigger and bigger; they've usually been around longer than most other companies, but that seems to be less the case these days. Mid-cap companies are $2 billion to $10 billion in market capitalization while small-cap companies may be as small as $250 million in market capitalization. Companies below that threshold are considered micro-cap or *pink sheet* stocks and are usually so thinly traded that it is hard to evaluate their true equity value. Many investors will favor holding large caps over small caps because the former are less volatile, they often pay out consistent dividends every quarter, and because so many people own them and watch them, investors believe their value is appropriately reflected in the stock's current price. Small caps may have fewer people analyzing them, a smaller base of owners, and their stock prices can swing wildly if the business does well or poorly for a given period; these are considered riskier businesses because they might be too small to survive a turbulent economic environment. Mid-caps share in elements of both large cap and small cap stocks; they tend to be on a trajectory toward large cap status by growing revenues quickly and hopefully streamlining costs out of their operations as they achieve scale, but they may have too much debt or post inconsistent profits.

VALUE VERSUS GROWTH

Another axis of evaluation that is very popular is *value* companies versus *growth* companies. Nobody of any authority really makes the determination, it's more like crowdsourced, but there are some general characteristics that apply. Value companies *tend* to be businesses that have been around a long time; their products or services are well known; and they have a very consistent or stable earnings profile; typically a moderate amount of debt because their cash flow is easily forecasted; and, they show steady margins and profitability. These companies often pay a dividend to shareholders, say something like 50% or more of the company's earnings each year. Investors like owning value companies because they know the business, want the stability, and enjoy reliable dividends.

At the opposite end of the spectrum, growth companies spur increased revenues every quarter with aggressive sales targets, and they constantly try to show new products or services that can generate even more growth in the future. These companies may not actually be profitable, but investors like the steady increases in revenues over time and a (hopefully) slower growth in expenses. Buyers of growth companies forecast a bright future where this company is dominant in their space and highly profitable with years of additional growth in market share and earnings. They often have less if any debt – since lenders tend not to like companies that can't make a profit: who's going to pay off the debt if you don't start making more money than it costs to produce your product or service? Again, there is no magic to a company being considered value- or growth-oriented, it is just an easy way for investors to categorize their view of a company's prospects and the potential for earning returns on an investment in that equity.

INTELLECTUAL STIMULATION

Equity markets are infinitely fascinating. Plenty of people see patterns in charts that track stock prices and invest accordingly.

Others believe it only makes sense to buy a company if its stock is priced at or below book value (net assets of the company divided by the number of shares outstanding). Still other investors check the price-to-earnings (P/E) ratio and will buy only companies that have a lower value than their peers or the index. Everyone can be right in the public equities markets... at least for a while. Nobody is always right with every investment, so when you do start investing in equities, mentally prepare to make mistakes and lose a little money occasionally. Learn from every trade, keep a journal of your thought process when you bought it, why you think the price will go a certain way and how you will reevaluate your position if things go differently. Good professionals do this constantly and then review their notes and keep another journal detailing what they learned from each of their trades and what they will do differently next time! The best pros review those second journals over a period of decades, develop a detailed philosophy for investing, build a business around it and mint *billions* for themselves and other investors who pay them *outrageous* fees to manage their Capital!

If equity investing seems interesting – and it most certainly is! – then try to constantly learn all about it. There are thousands of books written on equity investing; some are actually good! I can't even touch on the different theories and advice given for equity investing without writing a whole different book! They are all correct and wrong at the same time; there is no simple solution for getting equity markets correct – there is too much complexity in the market driven by too many individual motivations, and we haven't learned enough about complex systems yet to have *an* answer for predicting equity market movement, much less the *correct* value for any given company's stock price. But you *can* participate in reasonable, rational and appropriate ways to enhance the returns on your capital, prudently invested and well-diversified, to help you achieve your financial goals, moving you that much closer to fulfilling your purpose in life.

CHAPTER 13: THE PRIVATE MARKETS

Everybody wants to know what goes on behind closed doors... well, curiosity killed the cat, as they say, so be careful what you ask for! Also, get yer mind outta the gutter! The stock and bond markets – equities and fixed income – are considered *public markets* because they produce public financial statements, company stock prices are posted, buyers and sellers can transact quickly and easily on the public exchange, and the space is highly regulated by government agencies, *many of them,* but the SEC is the primary overseer.

Private markets on the other hand are more *opaque,* meaning there is less information available to help determine what an asset is worth, who owns it, or what strategy is being used to generate returns. Although that doesn't sound like a very appealing list of investment characteristics, most *institutional investors* favor these kinds of investments because they often attract some of the most talented managers who can generate incredible returns without the nuisance of public company regulatory reporting and oversight. There are literally trillions of dollars' worth of investing activity that is largely hidden from public scrutiny!

The key aspect of private markets is the avoidance of certain regulations, the very things that make *retail or individual investors* more comfortable about the experience. Oh, there are still numerous regulations, and more every year, but their intent is to limit the accessibility of private market investments to very large, highly sophisticated investors who can understand the various risks involved and who are unlikely to make foolish investment decisions. Occasionally, books are written when big private investments go sour, like *The Caesar's Palace Coup,* and when brand name businesses are involved, like RJR Nabisco in *Barbarians at the Gate*. This space is highly entertaining while also quite instructive as to how large pools of capital are invested to generate enormous returns from buying businesses and also lending to other businesses. Private market investment managers involved in real estate and even hedge funds apply many of the same strategies individuals *can* do, but they do them on a much larger scale – entire office towers or millions of shares of a company's stock – and make changes much faster than individuals with limited funds can accomplish.

ANGEL INVESTING

Early in the life of an entrepreneur's business, it is considered to be in start-up mode; in fact, the businesses are often called *start-ups*. The *founder* has an idea and a passion for seeing that idea implemented in the economy. For example, think of a really cool app you recently downloaded on your phone: someone had the idea for that app, they wrote some code, showed their friends, enhanced that app with feedback, and then decided to sell it to a billion other people. Well, that's a simplistic view, but you get the idea.

As a founder, you must demonstrate a *prototype,* an early working version of your idea, and explain why everybody on the planet *needs* this idea now. To get your business started, you reach out to friends and family for money; "friends and family" is another term for *angel investors* because they give you an early boost and a lot of encouragement. *Professional* angel investors usually know a lot of people in various industries who might eventually invest in your company and become your partner once it has proven to be a good investment: you release a great product or provide an amazing service, customers are willing to pay for it, you grow the number of customers and the amount of revenue every month, etc.

Time passes, you hire more people who can enhance the product, reach out to new potential customers, resolve existing customer complaints, or develop entirely new revenue streams from your idea. Oh, and since someone has to keep track of all the money you're making and spending... bring in the professionals! Angel investors can be critical to help you get past the hardest parts of starting-up a business, especially if it grows quickly enough to become attractive to other, more established businesses who want to buy your business or idea. For an investment of cash in your business today, the angel investor might take something like 5%, 10% or 25% of your company's ownership, leaving you with the rest. If you sell 10% of your business at a *valuation* of $100,000, you get $10,000 and you still own 90% of your company, just like on the TV show *Shark Tank*. Fast forward one year and you've built a better product version and grew your customer base such that your company is now worth $500,000. Your investor's $10,000 is now worth $50,000 and your 90% is worth $450,000 – wow! After a lot of hard work and sleepless nights, you have fulfilled a life goal and you also have some financial reward to show for it!

VENTURE CAPITAL

When start-ups grow quickly and get to a larger size, say a $1 million or $10 million valuation, they need even more capital to keep growing. Usually, fast growing companies are so busy hiring people and launching new services and spending money on marketing that every sale only covers a portion of the cost to produce that service. This is OK if you have enough capital invested to cover those temporary losses as you continue to grow the business.

Let's say you're at that point and the business is now worth $2 million because you have 10,000 people paying you $1 every month to use your app. New customers join as quickly as old customers leave, so you need help getting to *the next level*. Your angel investor is stoked because her $10,000 investment is now worth $200,000 – that's called a 20-bagger or 20x return♪ – but your 90% interest in the company is worth $1.8 million! You just can't spend any of it because it is only a *paper gain;* you can't easily sell a piece of it to someone else like you can with publicly traded stocks. Your angel investor says she will find a *venture capital* partner (VC) for the two of you and *their* investment in your firm will give you some cash in your pocket and will give her some *liquidity* for her investment; she will *realize* her gains and no longer be a part owner of your company; she spreads her wings and flies off to find her next investment to shepherd to success. The venture capital investor is a slightly different animal: it is usually in the legal form of a partnership because the *general partner* has *raised capital* from outside investors in the private market, those institutions like pension funds, high net worth individuals, university endowments and charitable foundations who are trying to make returns on their capital. Each of *those* investors are called *limited partners* (LPs) in the venture capital *fund* because they have only contributed money expecting the *general partner*, with their expertise, to find excellent companies to invest in and to help those companies grow quickly.

Back to our example: the VC fund wants to be your partner and they agree to buy 25% of your $2 million business. They pay your angel her $200,000 and you get $300,000 for all the hard work you've put in so far... payday! Now the really hard work begins because the VC firm will create a *board of advisors* or *board of directors* and they will insist on professional accounting and *audited* financial statements and many other *standard business practices* that you might have avoided as a start-up. Remember, their goal is to help your business grow very quickly so they can generate huge returns for their sophisticated investors – they have a reputation to uphold! They will offer advice and introductions to other professionals to help enhance the product, improve your marketing and eventually build a business that is big enough to be bought *entirely* by another, larger company or else grow to be *so big* and popular that you can offer shares of the company to the public market in a process called *initial public offering* (IPO).

That's the game plan: you're still the majority owner of your business, but now you have really smart people with a lot of money invested in your business and they will tell you what to do, how to do it and how quickly they want it done, usually *yesterday*! It is possible, and in fact more typical, to go through multiple *rounds* of raising capital through the VC network, resulting in numerous funds that own a part of your business. You will probably sell chunks of your equity along the way, hopefully never through a *down-round* which means the company's valuation is lower than the last time you raised capital for it, but that's also pretty typical.

On average, angel investors expect to lose money on more than half their investments and maybe break even on most of the others, but if they get *one awesome, killer* investment, they can recover all their losses and still make a lot of money. Venture capital follows a similar approach, investing $1 million to $5 million in each of 100 companies. They also try to minimize losses on each investment but still expect to lose some money on about half their deals and make at least 2x to 100x on a few best ideas. This is a fascinating space with lots of risk, lots of cutting-edge technology and amazing, energetic founders with brilliant ideas and huge personalities. And, of course, there are hundreds of great books to read about entrepreneur founders, angel investing and venture capital; many of the biggest and most popular technology companies out there today have travelled this avenue of private finance – check them out!

PRIVATE EQUITY BUYOUT

The "going public" or IPO process can also work in *reverse*. Let's say your company eventually goes public by way of an IPO, you still own 25% of the company but it's liquid now because you can sell a few of your shares every day in the market if you wanted to, and things are humming along nicely. A few years later your board of directors receives a proposal from a *private equity* firm that wants to buy *all of the shares* in your company! At a premium of 25% to the highest value it's ever seen in the public markets! Why would a sophisticated investor with so much money ever *do* that!?

Like VC firms, private equity (PE) firms are usually partnerships that have raised *even more money* from some of those same institutional investors, usually on the order of *billions* of dollars per fund. These *buyout* funds look for maybe 20-30 different businesses to buy, streamline and improve, combine with other businesses in *adjacent markets* and eventually sell the now-much-larger business to even bigger companies or again float the restructured company shares to the public market in a new IPO.

The partners of a private equity firm, referred to as the general partner or GP, usually have significant experience running large businesses and growing them quickly by making operations more efficient, by introducing new products more quickly, by hiring sharp marketing professionals who can advertise and make potential customers want to buy whatever they are selling, and very importantly, they use a lot of *leverage*, or *financial engineering*, to enhance returns to their investors. Leverage is debt. If you control a big asset like a business or a house with only 20% equity, that means the other 80% is borrowed money. If the asset goes up in value because sales and profitability are growing, leverage is great since you are making more money to pay off that debt and your equity capital is gaining value at the same time. The reverse is also true: too much debt, high interest costs, slowing sales, poor profitability... at some point, the lenders can force the company into bankruptcy and fight over the *residual value* of any assets left. Any existing equity can be wiped out entirely. These are the risks, but PE firms are expert managers and financiers who are rewarded by their investors for generating very strong returns using all the expertise they have learned over many decades in business.

The GP managers of the VC and PE funds discussed so far are paid fees by the investors in the fund, called limited partners or LPs, for managing their money, usually on the order of 1.5% to 3% of the capital *committed* by each LP. Think about that: if the GP raises a $2 billion fund and earns 2% *every year* for the ten-year projected life of the fund... that's $40 million times *ten years,* $400 million. Just for getting the capital to invest. OK, the *average* capital balance isn't really $2 billion for the *whole* ten years, but that management fee is intended to cover all the operating expenses of the fund, mostly the general partners' salaries, office rent, private jets and other various expenses of managing the fund. Now, the *real kicker!* The GP *also* earns a 15% to 25% *incentive or performance fee* for the combined profitability of all the fund's investments, usually paid out as deals are *realized* or sold.

The drawback to investing in VC or PE funds is that your committed capital is stuck in that fund until all the investments are realized. Investors get *distributions* whenever the GP decides they can do so without harming their investments. When a fund is structured to last at least ten years, sometimes those investments aren't realized and fully distributed until twelve, fifteen or even twenty years later! Limited partners have few rights to demand their money back, so once you commit to a private fund, you're in it for the duration... unless you want to sell your interest in an LP secondary market swimming with sharks looking for huge discounts on *their* investment to take you out!

In our example where you had an angel investor and VC firm help you grow big and go public via an IPO, let's say a buyout fund offers a $3 billion price to control the entire company you founded. Assume you still own 25% by that point so you get $750 million and a retirement party'. Congrats! The buyout fund improves the business with new executives, adds some debt, combines a few other smaller businesses, and accelerates the development of a few new products.

In about five years, they *shop* around to find a buyer for this bigger, better managed firm and discover another company willing to pay $10 billion. The sale results in a profit of $7 billion and the GP gets to keep a performance fee of 20% which equals $1.4 billion. That is a successful deal: the investors are happy, the GP's employees are happy, and you're still trying to figure out how to invest your $750 million now that you are a high net worth (HNW) individual. Actually, you would be considered an *ultra-HNW,* so you can now form your own endowment or foundation or invest as an *angel* in other companies! Maybe see if that PE firm will let you invest in their next buyout fund!

The numbers involved in private equity are staggering: trillions of dollars of existing investment, hundreds of billions of available capital to deploy and hundreds of billions of profits made for investors and investment managers alike. Also, there have been billions of dollars *lost* on individual investments that go pear shaped, a euphemism for sideways, which is another euphemism for "oops." Plenty of private equity GP's trying to make a name for themselves make a few too many bad investments or don't generate high enough returns from good investments to keep LPs interested in their next fund, so they fade into obscurity or never end up winding down their last fund: "welcome to the *Hotel California,*" sang the Eagles! Watch the news and read some biographies of these companies ...riveting stuff.

PRIVATE LENDING

Private lending is a relatively newer space that has developed over the last few decades because private deal sizes are so large and the amount of debt so big, that one or a few *regulated banks* just can't get it done on their own like they used to. Remember back to your savings bank that took your money as deposits and lent that money to other borrowers? They are regulated. Private debt funds came into existence to meet a need for private businesses who wanted to borrow more money than those regulated banks could lend; the private debt funds are not as highly regulated. This led to a *shadow banking system* because there is much less information about their lending, rates, terms and exposure to different kinds of borrowers. Where do private debt funds get their money? The same institutional players we discussed earlier! There are also *business development companies* (BDCs) that are essentially publicly traded funds allowing retail (small) investors to participate in the private lending space. Individual investors buy or sell shares in the BDC, a company that lends money to privately held, large companies.

There are thousands of companies that might have $25 million to $100 million in annual revenue or earnings, and they are often trying to grow quickly and get big enough to *go public*. One way to do that is to borrow their way to growth by buying a competitor or opening new locations or investing in a new production line or expanding into another country. All those actions are risky, but private lenders can charge higher interest rates and include various restrictions in the loan documents. They might also demand *extra security* by obtaining a *lien* or other *collateral* on existing assets of the business. They might also demand *warrants* or *options* to acquire equity ownership at a discount so, if the business enhancements go well the lender can profit both from interest income and from equity appreciation. These are huge pools of capital, lending out tens of millions or hundreds of millions for each loan at 10%-15% interest rates, hoping to get repaid quickly. Once a loan is *underwritten* and *advanced* to the borrower, the lender often sells off big chunks of the loan to other investors in a *syndicate* or club of other investors. There's even an index that tracks these kinds of loans called a *leveraged loan* index. So, yes, debt is a big, big business even in the private markets. If you are saving and investing, you can eventually participate in these kinds of compound interest opportunities; otherwise, you might end up a borrower, and investors will earn some great returns on your financial *illiteracy*.

INSTITUTIONAL REAL ESTATE

If you think buying a house requires a lot of capital and debt, think about a huge apartment complex, or a mall, or an industrial warehouse, or a high-rise office tower, or a fancy hotel. These are *commercial properties* that are usually owned by *private real estate* funds. Just like a mutual fund or private equity funds, there are GPs who specialize in buying, managing and selling big properties. Investors pay these investment managers an annual fee based on the amount of their investment in funds structured to buy properties, obtain mortgages on the buildings at the lowest possible interest rates, and collect rents from the tenants of those properties. With any money left over from operations after improvements, the manager pays a dividend to each of the owners of that property fund. Individuals often do this in a smaller way on their own by investing in a few single family or duplex rentals, maybe buying a strip center or owning a commercial building with a laundromat and donut shop. Some private real estate funds exist only to underwrite huge mortgages on the largest of properties – they don't actually own the underlying real estate, just the mortgages attached to it. Quite a few of the largest real estate funds have converted from a private fund to become publicly traded *real estate investment trusts* (REITs), so now individual retail investors, not just institutions, can buy shares of SPG, PEG, OPI and BXMT. Look up those tickers and read all about those companies, they are fascinating!

OK, back to the private real estate funds! Performance of these funds is usually tracked by an index called NFI-ODCE (pronounced like *odyssey*), which is a market cap weighted tracker for properties considered "core" real estate, which just means stabilized operating properties. Most investors like *core equity* real estate funds because they own the underlying buildings in the fund, hence *equity*, so they participate in any increase in the value of the property and the fund's shares increase in value. These kinds of properties also have reliable cash flows (net rental income or funds from operation) and return profiles (buildings in good locations generate cash and increase in value over time). Pension funds like investing in core equity real estate funds because they accommodate huge amounts of capital while generating constant dividends and *capital appreciation* with reasonably low volatility or risk. But *redeeming* an investment from some of these funds often takes quite a while – most fund documents allow only a limited amount of the fund to liquidate, usually over multiple quarters. Even this is only possible because the underlying investments are generating cash every month (unlike a VC or PE fund that may only realize cash inflow when they sell an investment or float an IPO).

Another real estate fund category is called "value-add" which means the properties need additional investment beyond just the purchase price to improve operations. These funds target significantly higher returns, say 15% - 20% each year, because they engage in riskier properties. For example, a fund manager might buy an apartment complex and update each unit; or convert an apartment tower into condominiums for sale; or *reflag* a Motel 6 to a more expensive, swanky brand like Embassy Suites. Well, OK, maybe *swanky* is a *little* generous...

HEDGE FUND' STRATEGIES

Well, earlier I said I'd cover *hedge funds* and it is truly a wild part of the investment landscape, so here goes! Probably best for your financial health if you *do not try these at home*. There are so many different strategies employed by managers who offer *hedged investments* that it is unfair to lump them all together in this category; it's more of a *misfit* category of investment *styles* rather than a *homogenous* asset class. Try this: if hedge fund land were a country, consider each of the different strategies discussed below as a different state. Some strategies are so similar, they have a "north" state and a "south" state (shout out to the Dakotas and Carolinas!), others are so popular they proportionally represent an investment amount the size of Texas or Alaska. Similarly, each strategy has its own colloquial uniqueness but none of the broad characterizations are fair; still, it helps frame a fascinating space for investments that you will undoubtedly hear about over time.

Earlier, we touched on long-short investing which is just one of many *equity hedged* approaches that includes long bias, relative value, short only, market neutral and directional strategies. Hedged equity has historically been the largest hedge fund segment and was the earliest strategy used: buy some *good* companies long and sell short a smaller basket of *bad* companies. The category names simply try to distinguish the degree of offsetting, or short, positions used by the fund's portfolio managers to generate returns and manage risk or market exposure.

138

The hedge fund structure allows the portfolio manager *leverage* through a *prime broker* to buy more than $1 of stocks long or short for each $1 of capital available to the manager to invest. The most basic approach is to buy 150% (or 130% or 250%) of the investment fund capital *long*, and then *short* 50% (or 30% or 150%) of the fund capital. The result is *net market exposure* of 100% of the fund's capital base but a much larger *gross market exposure* due to leverage or borrowed funds. The manager must be right about the stocks that are short or else they could lose all the money in the fund. For example, when TSLA went from $100 to $450, plenty of managers were short (expecting the price to fall) and lost a lot of money, while their long holdings of F, GM or TM didn't go up enough in value to offset those losses. Managers who are *great* at identifying terribly managed companies or bad business models become *net short sellers,* almost all of their positions are *against that market segment.* They want the individual companies or indexes they are short to decline in price. These guys get a bad rep in the press, but they add discipline to the market and help *price discovery* by applying realistic – OK, maybe pessimistic – expectations to their valuation of companies' financial statements. This requires a lot of research and expertise in *financial statement analysis* but getting it right can be very lucrative for the portfolio manager since these funds often charge 1% to 3% management fees and 10% to 25% performance fees, just like private equity and venture capital.

Another interesting segment of hedge funds is called *event driven*. These managers look for specific upcoming events in a business and try to position their portfolio to profit from it. Sometimes it's a special dividend payment, or a legal battle, or a product launch, or a subsidiary spin-out, or an executive succession... There are dozens of corporate events that happen all the time and because public companies are regulated, they must report these immediately after or sometimes well in advance of the event. This strategy requires significant business ability and not just a little knowledge about regulatory rules, legal maneuvers, and possible outcomes. Some event driven managers *create their own events* by acquiring a significant percentage of the outstanding shares and then becoming *activists* in the management of the company by writing public letters or demanding *proxy votes* to get themselves elected to the board of directors.

Owning shares in a public company makes you an owner of that company. Owners are responsible for electing a board of directors to oversee the business strategy; they hire executives to run the day-to-day activities. Other significant decisions require owner approval through a process called *proxy voting*, usually held once a year, occasionally more often. Alas, as in political elections, most investors don't vote their proxy, so incumbents usually win.

There are some crazy stories written about activists and the companies they've "attacked" or "helped" depending on the author's perspective. The goal of an event driven strategist is to get a position – either long or short – in anticipation of the broader market of buyers and sellers *eventually* figuring out how to value an unusual event. If they're right, these strategies can make a ton of money very quickly, especially since they often magnify the capital in their fund 5x or 10x using financial leverage.

Arbitrage is another collection of states in hedge fund land, like the Great Lakes region or the Pacific Northwest. The idea for these strategies is to capture the slight difference between a highly likely future value and today's price. One of the most popular approaches involves trading a *convertible bond* issue compared to the price of the underlying stock. The other most popular approach involves potential *mergers* between two companies – sometimes announced and not yet formally approved by either company. Let's unpack these ideas.

Some companies, especially in high growth industries like biotechnology or software companies might issue debt that investors can *convert* into equity ownership shares of the company at some point in the future, say five or eight years after the bond was issued. Usually, the bond offering documents will specify a certain number of potential shares or else provide a per share dollar value. Any time before the bond is convertible – say, does this sound a little bit like a call option on equities? It should! – the price of the bond will go up and down with interest rates (if interest rates go up, the price of the bond will go down and vice versa) and it will also go up or down *depending on the price of the underlying stock.* That is what makes the arbitrage possible – sometimes the price of the underlying stock goes up tremendously and the bond holders have bonds that are worth *way* more than the bond's face or par value if converted into stock... but sometimes that conversion is not allowed to happen for a few more years. *Convertible arb* managers have methods for trading the bonds and the equity of these companies to generate returns while exposing their capital to little risk.

Alternatively, when a big company wants to buy another public company, the boards of directors usually negotiate a deal in private and then announce the sale price, terms and target *closing date* for the transaction. The *acquiring* company stock usually falls a bit in price on the announcement, but the *target acquisition* company stock price usually rises, almost to the announced purchase price. Why not all the way? Well, sometimes good deals go *sideways,* or government regulators think the combined company will have a monopoly, or there might be a credit crisis and nobody will lend money to complete the transaction... lots of things can go wrong so there is a risk that the price of the target company will fall back to its pre-announcement price.   Merger arbitrage managers actively trade both acquiring company and target company equities while keeping close tabs on the developments of the potential deal; they often make a few dollars per share, with very little risk. If there are potential issues with the deal, merger arb managers can be either long or short one or the other *or both* parties to the deal, depending on where they think values and stock prices will ultimately settle! There is a lot of money to be made in these trades without much risk, especially if new bidders make higher offers for the target company!

Distressed debt is another opaque corner of the debt markets in which very sophisticated investors, usually with years of investment banking and legal backgrounds, can deploy capital in the loans and bonds of companies that have *defaulted* on their debt. Sounds risky, why do that? Well, there is usually some value to the ongoing business or at least some value in the assets of the company, but most fixed income investors don't want to deal with the time and stress of working out a deal to get only some of their money back, so they sell the paper at pennies on the dollar and just move on. The distressed debt investors usually join creditors' committees through a bankruptcy process, haggle with other debt holders who may be *senior or subordinate* to their own debt *priority*, negotiate with the nominal equity owners now called *debtors-in-possession* (DIP, how apropos): they defaulted on their debt but still possess the responsibility for operating the company.

Eventually, a judge must approve a settlement agreement. Sometimes the agreement is to sell all the assets via *Chapter 7 liquidation* and pay the bondholders according to their *seniority*, usually with a small *haircut* to the principal amounts owed, and the original equity owners lose everything; that's a pretty bad outcome. In other cases, the company goes through what is called a *Chapter 11 reorganization* in which the debts are restructured but remain payable in the form of new debt. Most of the equity value is redistributed to former *junior or subordinated* debt holders *and new management*. New management is usually put in place by the lowest debt holders in the stack because they receive most of the new equity in the new company that emerges from the ashes of debt like a phoenix ready to soar again... or so they hope. Often, the senior secured loan holders get most of the value in newly created debt to replace their old debt; lower priority tranches of debt fight over *controlling interest* of the new equity. This space is extremely complex and fascinating but takes a lot of patience, creativity and... how should I say it... chutzpah! if you want to be successful at it.

Some extremely sharp investors invite many other smart investors under an *umbrella organization* and build out what can only be referred to as a *multi-strategy* hedge fund, or "multi-strat." As the name indicates, it is one fund where the individual portfolio managers *compete* for an internal allocation of the capital in the fund. A group of managers might pursue long-short equity investing and get 40% of the multi-strat assets to invest. Other managers of distressed debt or convertible arbitrage may each have 10% of the multi-strat to invest. Still others may trade fixed income relative value, short only equity or maybe a sector specialist builds a concentrated biopharmaceutical portfolio hedged with index shorts. Occasionally, the chief investment officer (CIO) takes separate positions in some of the best ideas for their own "center book" as a way to enhance returns.

Maybe a dozen top quality multi-strats exist in the business and they attract the best and brightest portfolio managers eager to prove their prowess. Investors will *never* have a transparent idea of what is happening *under the hood* because that is part of the strategy's *secret sauce:* how the money is allocated to each strategy and how profitable each strategy is will never be disclosed. Multi-strats can deliver very consistent returns *efficiently* because the chief investment officer of the organization combines complementary strategies to minimize various risks inherent in individual underlying strategies. In a similar way, *funds of hedge funds* (or hedge fund-of-funds) attempt to achieve similarly reliable returns of 8%-12% annually with very low volatility, say 4%-10%. Institutional investors love investments that have high return and low volatility because it means their capital is growing fast without assuming too much risk. Don't get me wrong – there is still plenty of risk in all these strategies, it's usually just not in the *average volatility* statistics that many investors obsess about.

Let's wrap up this overview of hedge funds with *global macro* strategies because these tend to have the broadest perspective in all of investing, and I personally think they offer some of the best investment insights that scratch my intellectual itch. Macro investors trade the most popular asset classes – interest rates, foreign currencies, government bonds, equity indexes and commodities – typically using very liquid derivatives called futures, forwards or sometimes options. Remember, derivatives allow the investor to use only a little bit of capital to control a big slug of assets and some of these strategies get massively leveraged, up to 5x and 10x *per side* of the trade. That means for positions that are long, they might have invested 500% of the total fund capital which is then *balanced* with different short positions also amounting to about 500% of the fund capital. That's a tricky concept to wrap your head around in currency space. Anyhoo, imagine building a financial model of the global economy and valuations for each stock market and government interest rate and currency and commodity. Probably it will take a computer simulation ("Hello, HAL? " ::Yes, Dave:: "Hey, buddy, can you lend me your artificial brainpower to structure some trades while

I go for a spacewalk?" ::Sure, Dave... be safe out there::)*. After years of tweaking the various forecasting models, it suggests you should buy the German DAX and the Japanese Nikkei and the S&P 500 but sell the overvalued FTSE 100, Singapore's Straits Times Index and, of course, the French CAC40* and MOEX Russia* cuz... socialism, really? Oh, and get a few hundred million worth of Brazilian reis (but short those soybeans, yuck!) and increase the ANZ currencies (both Australian and New Zealand) along with some Canadian loonies and Mexican pesos by selling a few hundred million euros (that whole common currency thing just makes no sense... talk about artificial intelligence). Then layer in some long live cattle against short lean hogs, short orange juice, and long coffee (obviously). Box spread the nickel and copper positions, cuz who knows when housing and EV will settle down again... also, lever up the crack spread between oil futures and gasoline/heating oil, but put in a calendar spread for natural gas... by golly, you might make some money this week! No kidding, that's global macro! These managers usually have forecasts and positions in many of the deepest, most liquid financial derivatives of the biggest asset classes traded in the world. Conversations with them are like a world tour with the CIA director as your guide.

Granted, hedge fund strategies are not likely to be in your investment portfolio any time soon, if at all, but now you know they exist. And knowing about them is only half the battle! Even amongst my professional peers, there is serious and often heated debate whether these strategies can reasonably be expected to play an ongoing role in sophisticated institutional investment portfolios. Many of these strategies are *constrained* by the size of their investable universe or the competitiveness of other portfolio managers with similar strategies. It is also not uncommon to read articles about regulatory scrutiny and episodic market interference, like a ban on equity short-selling or government intervention in the debt markets or FDIC bailouts of banks... all of which directly affect potential profits and losses for various hedged strategies!

For now, though, hedge funds and other private market strategies exist to the tune of trillions of dollars of investment capital. The returns they generate have compounded over decades, making early investors billions of dollars; almost as much money as they probably generated for the managers selling them! If your new-found literacy in personal finance, saving and investing sparks an interest in you to learn more, I cannot encourage you enough to explore a career in finance and investment. There are so many ways to apply your knowledge, earn tremendous income, generate phenomenal returns (and probably more than a few losses along the way!), but also many ways to help others along in their own financial journey. It has been – and continues to be – a rewarding and intellectually stimulating pursuit for me. And it all started with decisions to spend less than I earn, save for a rainy day, invest for tomorrow and manage my Capital to compound returns over a few decades. What a fun adventure! I hope the bug has bitten you, too! May this be only the next step in your life-long journey pursuing excellence of purpose!

CONCLUDING REMARKS AND ENCOURAGEMENT

Well, this book maybe rambled on a bit longer than I anticipated, sorry about that. There is just so much to learn about money, and we just haven't figured out a great way to teach everything you need to know at this stage in your life. Most of my professional colleagues in the finance industry will skim this book and say, "well, that's just common knowledge," or "everybody knows this stuff already," or my favorite "but this is just scratching the surface – there's so much more to the story!" Absolutely! There *is soooo* much more to the story! But as a teenager, getting your first job and thinking about more expensive toys and signing up for your first credit card... where do you learn all these critically important things to manage all that responsibility? If your parents learned these lessons, maybe they taught you, but I have met many parents my age who *still* do not understand even the first few introductory chapters yet! They float through their careers, wondering why it is so hard to save money and yet everybody else they see has a shiny new car, a big expensive house and pretty handbags... with darling shoes! People show off things they adore and want others to notice, but *nobody* walks around showing off how much *debt* they have or how *little* they have saved in the bank.

Unfortunately, many parents cannot teach their kids these kinds of lessons because they haven't learned them yet for themselves. This little book lays out some *very* big picture ideas: what money is, how it can be used, and ultimately (I hope) makes the case that money is not the end goal. If you go through life trying to make more money just to compete with your view of others' success or what the advertisers want you to believe, your life will be wasted. Aspire to do so much more and make a greater impact on others' lives!

If you learn how to maximize the money you *do* make, it can help you achieve that impact faster and more powerfully. When you understand and manage deductions and taxes from your paycheck, you get to keep more of what you earn. Now consider how you *want* to spend the money you make after you cover your basic *needs* and put that in your budget. If you plan for big purchases, you won't need to borrow and take out debt to buy those things. In fact, banks and others will *pay you* to save your money! As early as *now!* start planning for retirement, even if you *think* you *want* to work sixty more years – and depending on your career, you probably could. However, you do not get to decide when you lose your job and can't find another employer; if your entire identity is wrapped up in that job, it might hurt emotionally for a long time. But that's not the end of the world if you have saved diligently your entire life, invested wisely and learned how to generate your own income from acquired assets!

You will enrich your life and your awareness of the world by reading about investments and paying attention to the stock markets and interest rates. You will be a smart world traveler who can linger in exotic locales for an extended stay because you know when a currency is *cheap* compared to your own *strong* dollar. As companies sell you something you love or provide an outstanding service, you will be able to grab a share of that well-run business and take part in its success.

Ultimately, my hope in writing this book is that you learn the language of money, that you become financially literate. Your newfound freedom from the stress of money will let you begin to dream about the purposeful impact you want to make in this world. You can invest for one impactful goal; or you can give away your savings to deserving causes; or maybe establish a foundation to make ongoing, lasting impacts that reflect your own life's purpose. You get to dream. You get to choose. Let this be an encouragement for you to start strong by managing your money well and then pursue your purpose in life without the nagging stress of money. Finally, share your knowledge, tips and tricks with the next generation and all your peers and neighbors because it is *so* exhausting to try and keep up with the Joneses. Trust me, they're tired, too!

APPENDIX A: THE DETAILED BUDGET TEMPLATE GUIDE

This book's QR code (page 49) allows you to download an Excel file with various worksheets used throughout the book; the hard copy budget detail is printed at the end of chapter four as a reference. And, while this might not be *anyone's* favorite section, it is nevertheless *the most* critical component of your overall literacy in personal finance. You really do need to understand budgeting well enough to create your own *and then* modify it to accommodate your unique circumstances. So, let's start with the "Budget Input" tab and work our way through the entry fields, calculations, and finally the "Budget Output" tab.

The template is set up to accommodate a semi-monthly, twice a month, pay schedule. Most of my jobs paid every two weeks, so there's a small discrepancy of two paychecks: annual salary divided by 24 (2x12 months) or 26 (52 weeks/year divided by 2). The cool thing about building the template in a twice-monthly format is the "extra" paycheck you get every six months... kinda like money *found in your couch cushions* because your budget ignores the day-and-a-half difference between paychecks. You get this "extra" paycheck twice a year that can be used to *pile-drive* debt or *sock-it-to-ya* savings! But OK, if you are a meticulous go-getter who wants to be, er, *retentive* about this minutia, feel free to recreate this template to account for *each individual paycheck* rather than the semi-monthly distribution shown here. It's a bit of work (I've done it, too) but it's a little more accurate which feels nice for... certain folks. It takes more maintenance to *keep* it accurate but it's good practice, and you'll develop some strong spreadsheet skills. Employers love it when their employees have boss-level spreadsheet skills!

For template purposes, input fields are in blue text and calculated fields are highlighted in grey so you aren't tempted to mess with them. If the cell is a negative value, like row nine (*Retirement Deduction*), it shows up red but the cell itself is not highlighted in grey, so you can change it to fit your specific situation. Also, it is often your choice *when* to pay bills; you can ask a card company or your landlord to set payments due on the first of the month or the fifteenth of the month and they will usually accommodate your request. The template is set up for you to move each line item to either the first paycheck column or the second paycheck column. Just remember, the whole point of this is to establish *an average monthly budget* which is then *extrapolated* (fancy word for *extended across the future*) for the next twelve months into what is called a "Cash Flow Statement" on the "Budget Output" tab. Check out that tab now: The top half is each month's first half cash flows, both income and expenses; the bottom half is each month's second half cash flows. A little bit further down on this "Budget Output" tab is a Balance Sheet section that converts your declining debts (from the bottom portion of the input tab) and growing assets (from savings and retirement contributions) into a *running tally* or *balance trend* so you can see the impact of all your hard work each month! I always loved trying to get a bigger balance than forecasted each month.

Remember: "Budget Input" fields are *an average*, but at the end of each half month, you will know the specific dollar amount of any paycheck deduction, expense or amount actually put into savings or investment. You can *hard code* that value on the "Budget Output" tab each time you get paid or pay a bill. The next period to the right will still reference the Input tab calculation while carrying forward the most accurate balance from the prior month total. Sleuth it out when budget balances don't tie with your actual statements; that will help you learn what else needs to be tracked better. You might need to add more line items!

Alright – back to the Budget Input tab. After your first month of working – let's call that January – you'll know how much your "Gross Monthly Income" is... let's say it's $3,600, which is $1,800 twice a month. If you have a side-gig, drop the first and second half earnings from January into the respective columns and the total will populate with the sum. Alternatively, if you have a whole slew of different income streams – rentals? loans to friends? other business income? tips from busking in the subway? – whatever it might be, just insert new rows if you want to keep them all separate and make sure the totals in column B capture the activity. The template is currently set to assume deductions total 25% of your gross income and side-gig income each period, but you can *fix* each of those amounts in column C and column D as appropriate according to your paycheck stub.

If you withhold *nothing* from your side-gig income, you will probably owe tax at the end of the year. If you withhold too much from your main job, you might be in line for a big tax refund next year. It is easier to manage the withholding from a main job than to estimate quarterly tax payments for a side-gig, so maybe run this out a year or so and see where you end up. As a legal precaution, I am not advising you on tax matters; seek the opinion of an expert here. Also, don't cheat.

<eyebrow emoji... you know the one>

Throughout the text of the book, I harped on the importance of contributing to your retirement account, so *of course* there is a place for that in your budget! Make sure row nine ties to your paycheck stub, and also include any employer matching contributions (also, increase your gross income by the same amount of the employer contribution to make the math work). Contributions show up as negative values since you don't get to spend this income, but the Balance Sheet section of the Budget Output tab makes sure to account for it as a positive: a negative on the *income statement* here is a *positive* for your long-term balance sheet *later*. And between now and retirement, it will grow to be an *even bigger* positive balance to include all those investment returns compounded over time!

Now to the Monthly Expenses section of the template. The first line item is called *tithe* or *charitable giving* because, based on empirical evidence, most people living meaningful lives are doing this. So, budget for it! If you are lucky, blessed, enlightened, evolved enough to make a reliable income, please feel obligated to pay that favor forward a bit for the benefit of others in need. The template uses a 10% figure, adjust it according to your habit, temperament or philosophy but realize it is or likely will be a permanent fixture in your monthly pattern of spending, so account for it early and often.

Rent or mortgage payments are usually due by the first of the month, so the template shows the amount coming out of the second half income to ensure that amount is sitting in your bank account when the check is written or before the ACH payment is sent. If you wait until your "first of the month" paycheck, the money might come out of the bank account before you get paid, then you're hit with an overdraft charge! Remember, this is a *planning* document, so you want to plan to fund any expenses *ahead of the due date*. Likewise, let's assume all your utilities are due the 15th of each month, so they show up as an expense to your first half monthly paycheck. The idea here is to capture a reasonable average, so if you know your electricity rate is going up by 8% next year, multiply last year's monthly average by 1.08 and use that value going forward. If you bought an electric vehicle, maybe check after the first couple of months to see what the increase is. Remember, this is a living document so you will need to review and adjust when things start changing in a *sustained* or *ongoing trend* to make sure the budget remains realistic and achievable.

This is a decades-old template, from back when folks still had landline phones. Maybe today's line item is monthly apps on your phone. Likewise, this template also shows "cable/internet" which is probably more accurately described as "internet/streaming apps". However you want to capture your expenses, adjust the headings to make sense for you and capture each expense.

The next few line items try to capture typical insurance coverage. Cars are the biggest, most common type, hard to escape, but you can shop around. If you don't have a car loan, you can usually omit certain kinds of coverage that are expensive and infrequently used. I have a whole philosophy on insurance (do you *really* think they'd be in business if they lost money *on average*?) but that's irrelevant for *your* budget. Include each item of insurance for which you're willing to continue paying a premium. Landlords encourage tenants to carry renter's insurance in case you or your friends damage their property; mortgage companies require certain minimum coverage of your home in case you blow it up... on accident of course. Mortgage insurance premiums are paid *by you,* so the lender gets repaid on the mortgage in case *you* default... how weird is that? Lenders require this kind of insurance if your down payment is less than 20% of the purchase price. Once your equity in the property is greater than 20% of its value, the lender will usually allow you to cancel this kind of insurance. This is one you should cancel as soon as you can.

Some folks pay for life insurance (if you are young, I believe this is statistically silly) or *supplemental health insurance* to, well, supplement or come in over and above the primary health insurance that is usually partially paid by an employer. Supplemental insurance is like having an uncle ready to pay your hospital deductible in case you forgot your wallet. Again, my philosophy is you might do better simply *saving* that amount each month in a special savings account rather than pay it to an insurance company, but that's my risk tolerance, might not be yours. No problem. Just account for each known, periodic expense and include it in your budget. Life insurance companies *love* to sell young people policies with investment options... do a lot of studying before you agree. I've known too many adults who have no idea what they got into and then can't get out without losing much of the value they thought they had accumulated over decades. My experienced opinion: life insurance isn't worth the cost. Feel free to read all about it and make your own decisions without being pressured by scare tactics from well-paid salespeople.

For those of you who already have credit card debt or car loans, row 24 begins the accounting for that monthly burden. Another section beginning at row 41 allows you to input today's principal balance owed, the interest rate charged, and a current *minimum* monthly payment. *Always, always* pay at least the minimum on your debts; otherwise, you incur additional charges. For this starter template, you'll notice *only* the minimum payment is being made for the car loan and credit card #1, but credit card #2 has *more than the minimum* payment being made – $100 instead of $45 – because it has the highest interest rate associated with it. I encourage folks to kill the most expensive debt dragon first, so that's where you should concentrate any extra cash flow each month. Don't cheat on this section: if you have multiple kinds of debt across many different store cards or student debt or whatever just list them out, find out the interest rate you're paying and the current balance. Start eliminating those millstones before you drown under the burden of debt. This budget is your best tool for figuring out how to do this! Once you list out every expense for every month and every debt and how much it costs you, you won't be able to ignore it any longer and you can begin to *plan* your attack rather than *react*.

The next two sections on the template – beginning with rows 52 and 58 – set up your Balance Sheet over on the Budget Output tab: checking and savings accounts; maybe they pay a tiny interest rate, or if you've already set up an outside brokerage account for investing, great, add that balance here. Some folks are granted stock options as part of their hiring process or career progress, so those can be added here or inside the retirement account, depending on how they are awarded. The *non-liquid assets* section includes things like Traditional IRA's, Roth IRA accounts, time deposits/CD's or variable insurance policies with an attached asset value... really, anything that is an asset should be included here. Make sure it flows into the balance sheet so you can watch their balances grow – either as you add savings and investment money to them, or as their asset values increase over time. You want to see these things over time because it triggers awesome neurochemicals in your brain that encourage you to keep up the good work! Also, it puts a smile on your face. And people tend to like other people who are smiling.

Now back up to Column F, row 40: Living Expenses. These are the kinds of expenses that are hard to nail down because they vary so much from week to week or even month to month, but we need to capture them, if only vaguely. This is where game play can be fun and rewarding: how much do you spend on food every day or week? How much do you *need* to spend? Have you figured out how many miles per gallon (mpg) you get when you drive? The typical range is between 12mpg and 33mpg; that's a big difference depending on your daily commute! Clothes aren't a *frequent* expense, but I'd be surprised if you didn't buy at least one thing every month... prove me wrong! How about restaurants or "food purchased not at home" ...include Starbucks, airplanes, convenience stores and vending machines. For a while, I limited this line item to $15 a day and found I could go out to lunch every day. Then I dropped it to $40 each week and realized that was too hard. Find something that works for you *and your budget* – don't worry about missing a few gatherings with friends if it isn't in your budget, or else bring your own refreshments when they go out! I have no idea how many living expense line items you need, the template includes one catch-all *miscellaneous*, so hopefully that helps.

Again, these living expenses will vary wildly from month to month so find a *close-enough* average and then try to gauge whether you spend more in the first half or second half of the month. The template provides the example of someone who spends about one-third over the first half the month and two-thirds over the second half of the month, maybe it should be split equally or maybe you're really hard-core and spend it all during the first week and spend nothing the rest of the month. Figure it out, learn about yourself and manage your habits to conform with the budget – because I believe it's easier to change behavior when you have a plan. If you don't want to change behavior, then *just* be realistic with your budget and increase your earnings to accommodate your desired lifestyle. Did that sound a little harder than *just* changing your behavior? Hmmm, *yes*!

You'll notice after all this effort that your budget probably doesn't *balance* to zero – it definitely *shouldn't* balance to _less than zero_! Any extra money at the end of the month should go to build up your savings or else pay off the most expensive debts. It is OK to have your checking account grow if you know next month you need to buy a new suit or expect to have higher grocery expenses or need to buy birthday gifts. A great trend would be to see your checking account get above some target amount, like $1,000 at which point you might shove any extra amount into a special savings account at the end of the month. If *that* savings account is above your target, then go ahead and make a bigger dent in that expensive debt balance, or maybe pay off the smallest balance if it doesn't entirely delete your safety net of savings. This is a *looong* process♪, so it is fine to show slow and steady progress; then reward yourself with a small luxury once you've eliminated a huge burden! Get that extra scoop of ice cream or invite your friends to a movie or out to eat, just *make sure it's all within your budget!*

Flip over to the Budget Output tab now. Notice each months' first half income and expenses at top and second half income and expenses below that... just as you put them in. But there is another line item at rows 26 and 51 for those *unplanned expenses* that hit you out of nowhere. Any month you get hit with one, drop those in and see what it does to your budget – hopefully not much since you've been building up a savings account. Try this exercise and see what happens: pretend you are hit with two new tires in column I – bam, $800 for asphalt bubble cushions. Sounds like a luxury, but it really isn't. What happened? Not much, just a minor reduction to your savings! In fact, you had more than enough in just your *checking* account to cover an *unplanned* expense that would have had other folks thumbing a ride to the office in Chester's old Yugo with the weirdly sticky seats and non-functioning seat belts, so embarrassing! Again, the idea here is you are budgeting a plan and when unplanned things happen, you can tackle them in stride like Jason Bourne and keep on moving forward. Yeah, maybe you work a few extra hours for more income or cut out some luxury expenses for a bit while you rebuild your savings, but you *didn't* get sideways on your budget, you *didn't* take out more debt or borrow from mom-and-dad... you're an adult now! You're financially literate! You're the *bomb!* How *cool* does *that* feel!? Better than a sticky Yugo', I can assure you.

Check out rows 25 and 50 which show a negative savings amount, that's weird right? Well, that is just a calculated field that says, "reduce the net income by *all other expenses* incurred for the period and shove the difference into monthly savings (row 67)." Not super helpful, author, but thanks for trying. Hang with me! Every dollar has to go somewhere, right? If you don't *subtract* savings as a kind of expense line item, then it just hangs out with nowhere to go. This template accumulates that amount into the monthly savings row 67 and allocates that amount to either the checking account or a savings account. The checking account is set up to *want* two months' worth of expenses as reflected on Budget Input tab, cell B32. That starts off as $1,440 so the checking account will accumulate the monthly savings amount until it has $2,880 at which point any further savings get shoved into the savings account. I got lazy and set the savings account to accumulate any surplus cash until it, too, was two months' worth of monthly expenses, but you can play with the formula to make it equal to four- or ten- or twenty-two months' worth of expenses if you want. That way, you'll have half a year, one year or two years' worth in liquid assets in case of emergency. (You *did* read that part of chapter seven in the book, *riiiight*? <eyebrow emoji> ...again.)

The reality here is that you would probably start paying down that 18% credit card, and then that 12% credit card before getting savings up quite so high, and even before setting up an investment brokerage account until those debt balances were slaughtered... (too visual? Too bad, makes it memorable!). With access to the template formulas, you can see how to bump the flow of *excess cash* from one line item to another. Adjust each of these to suit your needs and your interim goals. For another example, you'll notice I have "hard-coded" $100 contributions into a Roth IRA account at row 74, again, just to establish the habit of constantly contributing to things with the potential to compound returns for the next fifty years plus. Review the compound interest tables to see what a $100 contribution and 10% returns will do after 50 years... *righteous! Party on! Excellent!*

Last thing before you sell this book to a friend and recoup some of your cost... that would be the *financially literate* thing to do, after all! At the very bottom of the balance sheet, you will see the two *extra* net paycheck amounts that would occur if you were paid every two weeks rather than semi-monthly. You can do anything you want with this money since it isn't technically *budgeted*, especially if it has been super hard getting these habits going, or maybe you just need a treat as a reward. Fine. Otherwise, these could be used to accelerate the death sentence for remaining debt or rebuilding that savings account balance after a particularly nasty setback with unplanned expenses. In the best of all worlds, it goes toward investments, gifts or charity to help others less fortunate than you. It's nice to have options and now that you have the discipline to create, review and adjust your budget... you now have extra cash to pursue your purpose! That's been the whole point of this book: giving you tools, insights, and forward-looking perspective to maximize the utility of money so you can achieve goals, gain knowledge, apply wisdom and pursue your life's purpose. Hopefully you've set a super-aggressive target because you now have all the advantages to make the most of anything you earn. Share your experience and encourage the next generation to become even more financially literate and purposefully motivated than our generation ever has been!

APPENDIX B: GAMES PEOPLE PLAY

OK, probably my favorite appendix *EVER!* Well, I still kinda like the one I was born with, too, but it's hard to play with that one. Anyhoo... this is a list of games that I love playing with my family, and anyone else who will spare me the time. I grew up playing some of these as a kid and they still hold some kind of magic over me. Not only are games fun but those I've curated here also have a lesson to teach or some other financial reference. Sure, I wish I could convince the publishers of these games to throw me some swag for suggesting them, but I believe they are so helpful to people trying to develop good financial habits that I'm willing to just promote them for free!

ACQUIRE
Who doesn't love a game about starting your own company and then having it acquired by larger companies?! Luck is in the draw since the board is a matrix with one tile per square, but it's easy to start a company – you only need two adjacent tiles. I also (ruefully) appreciate the limitation of buying a maximum of three shares per turn; it's a great simulation of constrained investment resources (i.e., cash). The goal is ultimately to own more of the most expensive company, but to achieve that it's easier to start *and maintain* the majority share of ownership in a few smaller companies that get... *ACQUIRED!*

CASH FLOW 101
Yes, Robert Kiyosaki designed/underwrote this game, and his books are great for a lot of people; yes, I've read them and many of the ideas are good for starting out. I guess my only caution is to not get carried away with someone else's investment philosophy unless

you've fully considered how appropriate it is for you, in today's environment, with your level of experience and connections. Regardless, the games are great from the standpoint of portraying realistic life situations and typical investment options available to folks with different income- and asset levels. The "worksheet" is overwhelming at first, but when my son was six or seven and we started playing, we quickly developed a short-hand way to keep track of "passive income goal" as well as "assets owned." It's nice that they simplify to a few real estate deals, business start-up options, some gold plays, various stocks (with different volatility, so that was impressive) and other random (bad) investment options. The rat race concept is viscerally clear and "doodads" has been ingrained as a family code word – we never want to own a boat! Also, get downsized once or twice and you'll understand the entirety of chapter seven on a whole new level. While the options for "winning the game by achieving your dream goal" may be dated... it all works to teach great life lessons! My son was hooked the first game we played, and he beat me by the third game; I even audited him! Yes, he was still six or seven years old. I say he got a better job card than I did, so that's my excuse.

CASH FLOW 201

Yeah, once you get good at the long only game and know which price to buy the equities and which real estate deals to buy, how do you *up your game*? Well, add options, shorting and development opportunities, of course! This version is another level of more complicated but, again, the parallels to reality are so neatly drawn! My son gets so excited when he pulls a card that lets him short a ridiculously expensive stock even as he's high-fiving me over the gain he just made on the long side of owning that stock. When we play, he and I don't avail ourselves to the leverage allowed by the rules, nor do we lend or borrow from each other to access card opportunities, but that's probably more a function of the fact that we are the only two who play it; the ladies refuse to join us since we tend to get ...well, a little competitive? Unruly? Animated? It is a well-designed game for introducing teens to equity and real estate investing, long-short positioning, options and more (including multi-level marketing which I will again vehemently oppose, though it is an undeniably lucrative path to take in the game). Of all the games discussed here, the Cash

Flow board and expansion set are by far the most expensive... I also believe they are most specifically *on target* for advancing financial literacy among teens and their families. And tons of fun to play!

COVER YOUR A$$ETS

Cheeky, right? Might be why my son bought this card game for my birthday. Super simple to learn but a little hard to play with too few or too many players since the rules of play change significantly, but I can appreciate why it was designed in different ways for different numbers of players. The idea is to accumulate the most three-card combinations that add up to the highest total. I could quibble about the kinds of "assets" included, but they are fun and readily identified by everyone as "something I'd like to have" that might be worth more someday. Rounds are usually pretty quick, so "best out of three" is how we play it. Makes a nice gift for holidays with extended family and gets everybody else thinking in terms of "why not me?"

THE GAME OF LIFE

This one is better if you have younger siblings, I think. It strikes me as colorfully childish yet appropriately educational. We prefer to play with a 10-sided die rather than the oopsie-prone wheel of chance, but don't let that deter you. The game offers a choice to go to college or begin a career – with only one extra payday? Come on! You can start a family and have expensive children, buy a house, consider insurance, get speeding tickets, and invest in a number (even if it does work more like gambling)! And the goal? Retire wealthy! Great as an early introduction to major discussion topics for developing a life plan like education, careers, expenses and big income opportunities all leading to "what's retirement?" and how can I win at that! Probably no game better for building good habits early; well, except for maybe...

MONOPOLY!

Everybody has played this and it is still one of the classics that deserves constant relaunches! The original "Streets of New York" version is still my favorite. We generally avoid using Free Parking as a lottery to goose others' income from taxes, fees and penalties and we don't allow gifting of money from player to player... and kids get it! They love the action, the randomness of good or bad Chance and

Community cards, the thrill of owning all two, three or four spaces of a utility, neighborhood, or railroad. It's always illuminating to see who plays close to the edge and who plays too conservatively to ever win. Dust this one off and get back in the game... literally!

PIT (CORNER ON THE MARKET)

Right, this one is definitely more obscure, but I loved how animated and loud all the adults used to get when I played this as a kid attending potlucks and holiday get-togethers. My wife and I used to yell frantically at our parents and her siblings to trade commodities in hedonistic bliss trying to get a "corner" on wheat, oranges, coffee or soybeans (yukka pukka! I always traded those away first and often!). Back then I didn't understand the significance of the wild cards, bull and bear, but OK, I see it now. So, if orderly turn-taking or board games aren't your thing or maybe you just like to shout down your relatives, this game will probably scratch your Chi-town pit trading itch – as long as you have big enough shoulders!

Z GEN SPIN-OFFS?

As you can tell, I'm still old-school. I imagine there are many apps designed to be entertaining and yet convey some financially literate message or concept. I just don't know of any. Surely, there are games that teach economics and I know a few large businesses have developed addictive ways of gamifying investment and speculation (Roaring Kitty is again making news!). My bias would be to treat these apps cautiously and make sure they don't conflict with your budget or otherwise encourage speculation and gambling. Investing is not about memes or rapid-fire day trading for most of us individual investors. And if you are required to buy the app or pay a monthly fee... I'd definitely put it in the "want" column rather than the "need" category. Invest that money into shares of the game designer if you think it is so cool!

APPENDIX C: THE UNOFFICIAL SOUNDTRACK

Why don't books come with a soundtrack, huh? This was my feeble attempt at an easter egg hunt (a la *Ready Player One*) throughout the book. Also, my brain is wired to think in terms of songs, movies, and books... or maybe I'm just wired from too much coffee. Your musical tastes are sure to differ from mine, but hopefully some of these won't be too painful... enjoy!

Bubbles – *Kitties Are So Nice*
Sonia Jones – *Brian*
The O'Jays – *For the Love of Money*
Alt J – *Hard Drive Gold*
Ray LaMontagne – *Beg Steal or Borrow*
Daisy Chainsaw – *Love Your Money*
ABBA – *Money, Money, Money*
Primus – *Jerry Was a Racecar Driver*
Josh Turner – *Soldier's Gift*
Dolly Parton – *9 to 5*
Walter Mitty and His Makeshift Orchestra – *Community College*
Pet Shop Boys – *Opportunities*
The Beatles – *Taxman*
Dire Straits – *Money for Nothing*
The Beatles – *You Never Give Me Your Money*
Barenaked Ladies – *If I Had a Million Dollars*
Taco – *Puttin' on The Ritz*
StoryBots Songs – *Budgets*
Weezer – *Beverly Hills*
Orbital – *Pants*

Bill Kirchen – *Hot Rod Lincoln*
Kenny Rogers – *The Gambler*
Juno Reactor – *Pistolero*
Moby – *James Bond Theme*
Carter USM – *Sheriff Fatman*
The Overtones – *Gambling Man*
The Smashing Pumpkins – *Bullet with Butterfly Wings*
Camper Von Beethoven – *When I Win the Lottery*
The Dead Milkmen – *Dollar Signs in Her Eyes*
Cake – *Short Skirt / Long Jacket*
Jane's Addiction – *Mountain Song*
Reel Big Fish – *Sellout*
Juno Reactor – *Masters of the Universe*
Richard Strauss – *Also Sprach Zarathustra, Op. 30*
Parov Stelar – *The Paris Swing Box*
Red Elvises – *She Works at KGB*
Future Sound of London – *Papua New Guinea*
Cake – *The Distance*
Left Wing Fascists – *I Drive a Yugo*

ABOUT THE AUTHOR

Following business school, Brian worked in real estate finance and then institutional investment advisory work before representing a global macro and liquid alternatives investment manager. Throughout his career, Brian also coached young adults and professionals through topics of education, career development, budgeting, saving, investing, and launching their own businesses. Brian lives with his family in Bellevue, Washington; this is his first book... so please be kind.

If you are interested in hosting an interactive presentation of this book's lessons as a workshop for your conference or classroom, contact financial-literacy@stepintopurpose.co and discover how financial literacy can help you and your team achieve a greater purpose in all your life's goals!

www.ingramcontent.com/pod-product-compliance
Lightning Source LLC
Chambersburg PA
CBHW051425090426

42737CB00014B/2836